MEET ME AT THE BARN

DISCOVER YOUR LIFE'S PURPOSE AND EMBRACE YOUR HIGHER CALLING

MEET ME AT THE BARN

DISCOVER YOUR LIFE'S PURPOSE AND EMBRACE YOUR HIGHER CALLING

LAMARR K. LARK

ethos
collective

MEET ME AT THE BARN © 2024 by Lamarr K. Lark. All rights reserved.

Printed in the United States of America

Published by Ethos Collective™
PO Box 43, Powell, OH 43065
www.ethoscollective.vip

This book contains material protected under international and federal copyright laws and treaties. Any unauthorized reprint or use of this material is prohibited. No part of this book may be reproduced or transmitted in any form or by any means, electronic or mechanical, including photocopying, recording, or by any information storage and retrieval system, without express written permission from the author.

LCCN: 2023917426
Paperback ISBN: 978-1-63680-217-6
Hardcover ISBN: 978-1-63680-218-3
e-book ISBN: 978-1-63680-219-0

Available in paperback, hardcover, e-book, and audiobook.

All Scripture quotations, unless otherwise indicated, are taken from the Holy Bible, New International Version®, NIV®. Copyright © 1973, 1978, 1984 by Biblica, Inc.™ Used by permission of Zondervan. All rights reserved worldwide.

Scripture quotations marked RSV are taken from the Revised Standard Version of the Bible, copyright 1952 [2nd edition, 1971] by the Division of Christian Education of the National Council of the Churches of Christ in the United States of America. Used by permission. All rights reserved.

Scripture quotations marked HCSB are taken from the Holman Christian Standard Bible®, Used by Permission HCSB ©1999,2000,2002,2003,2009 Holman Bible Publishers. Holman Christian Standard Bible®, Holman CSB®, and HCSB® are federally registered trademarks of Holman Bible Publishers.

Any Internet addresses (websites, blogs, etc.) and telephone numbers printed in this book are offered as a resource. They are not intended in any way to be or imply an endorsement by Ethos Collective™, nor does Ethos Collective™ vouch for the content of these sites and numbers for the life of this book.

Some names and identifying details have been changed to protect the privacy of individuals.

Dedication

This book is dedicated to the memory and enduring influence of my beloved parents, Levoda "Madea" Lark and Jeffery Lark, Sr. Their love and wisdom shaped the person I am today, and I carry their legacy with pride and gratitude.

To my extraordinary siblings, who, as the pillars of our family, played a pivotal role in shaping my journey as the youngest of 11 children: the late Laura Lark-Brown, the late Jeffery Lark Jr., Alice "Dora" Rouse, Jean Lewis, the late Rosie Lark-McKnight, the late Attorney Edward Lark, Robert Lark, Sr., Virginia "Bonnie" Chism, Reed Lark, Sr., and Jamie Love. Your collective influence has been the bedrock of my strength and character.

A heartfelt thank you extends to my cherished brother-in-law and sisters-in-law, whose warmth and camaraderie have added immeasurable richness to our family tapestry. Also to all my amazing nieces and nephews, you have added an amazing joy to all of our lives over the years.

To my three incredible children, Lamarr Lark, II., Jasmine Greer, and Moriah Jacobs, each of you is a beacon of joy and inspiration in my life. Your unique spirits have added depth and purpose to my journey, and I am endlessly proud to be your parent. Special appreciation to my two wonderful sons-in-law for their love and support, contributing to the richness of our extended family.

Lastly, to the love of my life for 39 plus years, Brenda E. Lark—your unwavering support, understanding, and love have been my anchor through life's ebb and flow. This book stands as a testament to the shared experiences, challenges overcome, and the enduring bond we have built together.

Table Contents

Foreword by Chad Jenkins xi
Foreword by Peter "Trevor" Wilson. xiii
God Prepared Me For This. xv
   God Preparing People is a Biblical Tactic xvii
   On to Greater Things xix

Part One: Lost

Chapter 1: Searching. 3
   Trusting When We Can't See the Path 5
   Winter at the Farm 7
   We Needed Another Miracle 10
   Transformation at the Barn. 11
   Listening for Your Higher Calling 13

Part Two: Listen

Chapter 2: Learn 17
    Like a Child. 18
    A Journey Not a Destination. 19
    Learning Means Unlearning 20
    Lessons from the Barn. 21
    Learning to Connect. 22
    From Learning to Listening to Leading 25

Chapter 3: Inspire 29
    The Connection Team 31
    The Pivotal Part of our Team. 32
    Inspirational Teams from the Bible 33
    What to Do When Your Team Abandons You 34
    The Non-Inspirational Choice. 35
    The Greatest Source of Inspiration 39

Chapter 4: Serve 41
    Serving at the Barn 42
    Service Means Being Willing to Get Dirty. .43
    There Are No Excuses in Serving 45
    Fear Is Not a Reason to Avoid Serving 46
    Serving Involves Sacrifice 48
    Biblical Service 49

Chapter 5: Think 53
    Thinking about the Possibilities. 54
    Funding the Impossible. 55
    God of the Impossible. 58
    Too Big for Our Britches 59
    Take the Next Step and Let God Work 60
    Biblical Thinking. 62

Chapter 6: Encourage 65
    Encouraged by People Who Love Us 66
    Encouragement Directed at Fear................68
    Encouragement Transfers Strength..............69
    Encouragement Comes In Many Forms..........72
    The Ultimate Encourager 75

Chapter 7: Navigate..............................79
    A GPS for Your Life 80
    Following a GPS Takes Courage................82
    Adjustments Along the Route..................83
    Navigating Like King David 84
    Learning to Navigate at the Barn 86
    Let God Help You as You Navigate.............88

Chapter 8: LISTEN to Unlock Your Higher Calling...91
    LISTEN to Your Vision 92
    You Are What You Listen To 94
    Leaders Listen.............................95
    Making People Feel Heard 96
    Celebrate Your Higher Calling 98

Part Three: Limitless

Chapter 9: Meet Me at the Barn..................103
    Increasing Your GPA through Community.......104
    Actions Speak Louder than Words 105
    Mike's New Journey........................107

Small Group Discussion Questions

Session 1: Introduction and Chapter One
              God Prepared Me for This 113
Session 2: Lifelong Learners.....................116
Session 3: Find Inspiration 119

Session 4:   Self-Sacrificing Service. 121
Session 5:   Think About the Possibilities 124
Session 6:   Encouragement Helps Us LISTEN 127
Session 7:   Navigate Toward Your Higher Calling 130
Session 8:   LISTEN to Unlock Your Higher Calling . . . 133

Acknowledgments 135
About Lamarr K. Lark 137

Foreword by Chad Jenkins

In *Meet Me at the Barn*, Lamarr Lark shares a journey that resonates deeply with anyone who has ever strived to discover their higher calling in life. As an entrepreneur who has always sought to identify and cultivate the unseen potential in businesses, I found Lamarr's story particularly compelling. His narrative is not just about personal growth and faith; it's about the transformative power of seeing beyond the surface and understanding the deeper value in people, places, and experiences.

Lamarr's journey from a youth laden with responsibilities to a visionary leader in his community is a testament to the power of resilience, faith, and strategic thinking. His experiences, so vividly and candidly shared in this book, are a reminder of how challenges can be reframed as opportunities for growth and leadership. The barn, a central motif in his story, is emblematic of his ability to see potential where others might not, transforming it into a beacon of hope and community.

This book is not just a narrative; it's a blueprint for anyone looking to uncover their purpose and make a meaningful impact. Lamarr's life story is a powerful example of how faith, combined with a keen sense of purpose and dedication, can lead to remarkable achievements. His insights are particularly relevant for business leaders, entrepreneurs, and anyone aspiring to make a difference in their community.

As you delve into Lamarr's story, I invite you to reflect on your own journey and the 'barns' in your life waiting to be transformed. "Meet Me At the Barn" is more than just a read; it's an inspiration to pursue a life of significance, guided by faith and a deep understanding of your true potential.

—Chad Jenkins
CEO of SeedSpark,
Bestselling Author of *Just Add a Zero*

Foreword by Peter "Trevor" Wilson

I have known Lamarr Lark for most of my corporate life. I have been truly amazed by his fearlessness (i.e. faith), hope (i.e. optimism), and discipline. In a world dominated by noise and incessant chatter, where everyone seems eager to speak but few take the time to truly listen, Lamarr's first book, *Meet Me at the Barn*, emerges as a guiding light towards a more purposeful existence.

In this transformative book, Lamarr delves into the profound and often overlooked art of listening, unraveling the extraordinary power it holds in unlocking the doors to one's personal higher calling. The book is the epitome of what we now call human equity. Through captivating narratives, insightful anecdotes, and practical exercises, readers are invited on a journey to harness the transformative potential of attentive listening, not only in their relationships with others but as a powerful tool for self-discovery.

Meet Me at the Barn challenges the conventional narrative of success and fulfillment, urging readers to tune into the subtle melodies of their inner selves. By embracing their authentic identity, Lamarr contends, we can attune ourselves to the harmonies that lead us to a life lived on purpose.

This book serves as a compass, guiding individuals toward a deeper understanding of their true passions and values, and empowering them to orchestrate a life that resonates with authenticity and fulfillment. As readers embark on this journey of self-discovery through attentive listening, they will find that the cacophony of the world fades away, leaving behind a serene melody that beckons them toward a purpose-driven existence.

—Peter "Trevor" Wilson
Bestselling Author of *The Human Equity Advantage*

God Prepared Me For This

Where is it? I know I put it in there! I searched my pockets for the fifth time before I went inside with my head down. I couldn't look her in the face.

"I lost it, Madea," I said almost under my breath.

"Lost what, Lamarr?" I could hear the disbelief in my mother's voice.

"Daddy's check." I couldn't hold back the tears anymore. "I was sure I put it in my pocket, but I looked everywhere, and it's gone."

"Lamarr!" Madea's voice just made me cry harder. "Lamarr, you have to find that check."

"But, Madea, I don't . . ."

"It doesn't matter, Lamarr; you better go find that check. Get back on your bike, and don't come back here without it." She repeated herself as I closed the door. "You heard me, Lamarr, don't come back without that check!"

I was bawling by the time I got back to my bike. For two years, I'd been picking up Daddy's check every Friday, and on that particular day, I'd been upset because my friends had been picking on me. Everyone else was heading over to play basketball, but I had to run errands for my parents. I'm pretty sure twelve-year-old Lamarr had been careless with his dad's check because he was angry that he couldn't shoot hoops with his friends.

I'm the youngest of eleven. My oldest siblings called our mother Madea twenty-two years before I came along, decades before Tyler Perry made the name famous.

Madea was a nurse's assistant, and Daddy was a truck driver. By the time I was ten, I carried considerable responsibility. Every payday, I picked up my parent's checks and took them to my mother. Madea would get those checks ready for deposit and write the bank drafts to pay the bills. With everything in its own envelope, I would get back on my bike, ride to the bank to make the deposit, and drop off payments at the correct utility companies.

My parents worked really hard to take care of us, which also meant they weren't home much. But with so many older brothers and sisters, I had plenty of "moms and dads" at home. I've always thought that after raising so many kids, my parents felt they needed to accelerate my childhood and raise me differently than they raised the others. When I lost Dad's check that day, I knew I had let them down.

Still crying, I got on my bike and retraced my steps. I looked down every side street and walked my bike a good part of the way so I wouldn't miss anything. By the time I could see Dad's workplace, I knew it was hopeless. But as I stepped over the train tracks, I noticed an envelope fluttering several yards away. There near the rails. The tension eased from my body, and I sighed with relief: it was my dad's check. Thank you, Lord.

I sped back home, and when I handed the check to Madea, she simply said, "I'll bet you never do that again."

Some might question treating a ten-year-old like he's twenty-one, but God knew what He was doing. Unlike most children my age, I knew how to do the banking and pay bills. I understood the relationship between income and expenses. God used my parents to set me up for success and entrepreneurship. Before my eleventh birthday, I knew every person at the bank and had learned how to interact with adults—the perfect skill for a future pastor. On top of that, my ten brothers and sisters each had determined to make sure I did better than all of them. Dad and Madea always told us they worked hard so their children could have a better life. They taught me to believe Luke 1:37—"With God nothing shall be impossible." So, I grew up with these extremely high expectations of myself and a belief I could do anything I set my mind to. Despite the fact I got angry and frustrated every time I missed out on fun with my friends, I now realize my parents gave me a great gift.

God Preparing People is a Biblical Tactic

I'm not the first young person to be given adult-sized responsibility that prepared him for his future. Joseph was Jacob's twelfth child, and much like my parents, his father treated him a bit differently than the rest of his siblings. Did the attention he got as a child sustain him while he sat in an Egyptian prison? God gave him dreams so he could see his future. At seventeen, he became a slave, yet he didn't stop giving God glory and living for the vision God had given him.

Daniel lived at least seventy years after being taken from his home—from the beginning of the Babylonian exile until after the Israelites were released. So, when he and his friends stood up to the king's steward and refused the decadent food, he couldn't have been more than a teen—probably between twelve and sixteen.

Israel's King David began his life as a shepherd. Like me, he had several older siblings—seven brothers and two sisters. And like me, he started with some high-level chores at a pretty young age. When Samuel looked for the next king among Jesse's sons, David had been left alone to care for the sheep. Most scholars put David at fifteen or younger when Samuel anointed him Israel's future king, but since he was competent to be left alone in the field, we can assume he'd started taking on the responsibility at a much earlier age.

David's story demonstrates the way God prepares us. Alone in the fields, David learned how to play the lyre and developed his talent for songwriting. That opened the door for him to observe the responsibilities of a king firsthand while he played for the tormented King Saul.

David told Saul his battles against bears and lions prepared him to fight Goliath. And living in the hill country outside of Bethlehem got him ready to hide out in caves as he avoided Saul and built his following. Every step of the young shepherd's life developed qualities that would allow him to shepherd God's people as king.

And if you worry about David and me being given so much responsibility so early, read Samuel's story. The prophet might have been as young as three when he started serving in the temple. By the time he was eight, God spoke to him personally. And even though he wasn't a direct descendant of the high priest at the time, his childhood training set him up to take over after Eli's sons handled the office miserably.

I don't know if David and Samuel felt as frustrated as I did when they had to miss out on childhood fun, but I'm pretty certain they ended up as grateful as me once they realized the great gift they'd been given in the preparation phase of their lives.

On to Greater Things

The confidence my parents placed in me during my young years catapulted me to greater things. When I hit high school, I participated in sports and pushed myself to do well in school. I also joined an organization called the Distributive Education Clubs of America (DECA). Their goal is to prepare emerging leaders and entrepreneurs for success after high school. During my sophomore year, I heard my marketing teacher say something about officer positions outside our school, so I asked her about them. She explained that DECA had chapters all across Indiana and the United States and that there were state and national officers who made decisions for the organization.

"Could I run to be a regional officer?"

"We've never had an officer from our school. In fact, we've never had an officer from South Bend. So, if you're serious, I'll help you. I see something different in you, Lamarr."

I didn't know what she saw, but she helped me organize a campaign, and I began to learn a little about politics. That year, I ran for a regional office, and I won. The next year, I won a state office.

The leaders at the state level must have seen something in me because they started talking to me about running for a national office. There had never been a national officer from Indiana, and they thought I could change that. They helped me get support from high schools all across Indiana, and I asked my parents if I could go to Anaheim, California, for the national election.

With four days to campaign before the election, Dad, Madea, and a couple of my brothers and sisters took me to

California. At the Anaheim Convention Center, each state I would be representing interviewed me, and I had a chance to speak before each delegation. I met people from across the country, and by election day, I said to my family, "I might actually have a chance to win this."

In an effort to protect me from myself, Madea took me aside. "Lamarr, you have a lot of competition here. I want you to know–even if you don't win, I won't be disappointed. You've worked hard and made us proud. When they tell us the results, I don't want you crying and falling apart. You did your best."

"No, Madea, I'm gonna win this!" I truly felt like I couldn't lose.

"Calm down, son. I just want you to be prepared."

When they read the election results that night, and I walked up on that stage to accept, I saw Dad and Madea beaming. They looked like they were thinking *maybe all the work we put into this young man is beginning to pay off.*

That campaign and the next year were incredible experiences for me. I learned so much that I would use later in my life. And again, though I didn't realize it at the time, God was preparing me.

Just before we headed to California, I'd become a Christian. God had allowed a man named Sam Dalton to come into my life, and through his mentoring, I discovered what it meant to be a true disciple rather than a dedicated church-goer. Sam had a list of acronyms that helped me remember important Christian truths, and his walk mimicked Jesus' life in such a way that I knew I wanted what he had.

Like most new followers, my prayers were a bit self-centered. For instance, as we headed to Anaheim, I prayed, "God, I really want to win this. If you help me get this office, I'll do anything you ask me to—anything." I didn't really understand the magnitude of that prayer, but it was literally life-changing.

Growing up, I'd always planned to go to college close to home. After all, we lived in the college football capital of the world. I had my sights set on Indiana or Ball State, but my victory in California changed that trajectory. I decided I wanted to honor God with my college choice, so I picked a Christian school and enrolled at Grace College in Winona Lake, Indiana, about an hour from home.

I spent my days studying business and talking to my roommate about my dream wife. I prayed often for this mysterious woman. "God send me the right girlfriend and the person that could someday be my wife."

One weekend when I was home, my sister informed me she had found the perfect girl. You know older sisters—I really wasn't interested.

"It's a girl at church, Lamarr. You have to meet her."

I still wasn't ready for my sister to find me a girlfriend. But that weekend, she introduced me to Brenda. And as much as I hated admitting it, my sister got it right. When I told Sam I thought I'd found the girl God intended me to marry, he immediately wrote our names in his journal and started praying for us as a couple.

So much happened during the next couple of years. I joined the National Guard Officer's Candidate School to finish funding my education and missed Brenda desperately the entire time I was gone. When I returned home ready to go back to Grace College as a junior and marry Brenda, my parents were a bit skeptical.

To their delight, we both graduated. Brenda became a teacher, and I started looking for something in the corporate business world. I finally landed a position at a pharmaceutical company, not knowing at the time how much God would use this secular position to prepare me for the ministry He had planned for me.

PART ONE
Lost

1

Searching

Not All Who Wander Are Lost

For the next twenty-four years, I flourished at the pharmaceutical company. The first fourteen took me from trainee to vice president. I received promotion after promotion. Most would have called me extremely successful. I traveled globally and relocated my family three times. But through it all, I kept counting the number of years I needed to work before I could retire.

Retirement from this job started at age fifty or ten years of service. I started planning for that day during my first couple of years. Over and over, I told myself I would not work past my fiftieth birthday. I saved and invested, and as far as the world was concerned, success followed me around. But deep inside, I knew this career was just another time of preparation. I didn't know what God had in store, but I knew this wasn't my highest calling.

Throughout those years, my family attended church faithfully, and I held a variety of positions. Each time we moved, we found a new congregation to fellowship with, and I became intimately and deeply involved, often as one of the assistant pastors.

Around 2006, the congregation we worshiped with started to look for a place to build a new church. We had amazing plans. I lived in the world of corporate America, and I knew that God deserved something as elaborate as that avenue of my life would build. So, when we found a farm for sale, and the farmer's wife decided to sell it to us at twenty percent less than the asking price because a church was buying it, we felt like it was a gift from God. Our plan was to tear down the barn and the two old houses that sat on the land and build something modern and inviting. The architect's design was stunning. More than anything, I wanted to honor my Savior.

The market failure of 2008 really threw off our timeline. We had been confident that bigger and better would be the best way to give God glory; however, that financial crisis took several families out of our church as they moved to get new jobs. All the dreams for the farm looked bleak. Finally, the senior pastor at the time came to me and the other three families who had signed the loan for the farm and gave us difficult news. He felt like the Lord was calling him to a different ministry, and he left the four of us to decide what to do with the farm.

The crash had hit the other three guarantors hard. By 2009, they needed to move to take care of their families. "Lamarr," one of the other investors said, "there's no sense in dragging out the inevitable. We might as well just let this land go back to the bank."

I said, "No way. Not on my watch."

"Lamarr," another said, "this farm is going to destroy you."

I was an executive pastor by now, though the congregation had dwindled due to the extensive moves. Despite that, I decided that I was going to hold on as long as I could. Letting the bank foreclose would mean all our credit ratings would take a huge hit, and I still felt like God had plans. Plus, I had promised them when we signed the loan I wouldn't allow this mortgage to damage any of our credit scores. So, I encouraged the others to walk away with no hard feelings, and I kept making the payments, waiting to see what God would do.

At the same time, Brenda and I realized we had everything in place for me to leave the pharmaceutical company. I knew corporate America wasn't the plan God had for me. Unfortunately, I still had two children in college, our household bills, and now the mortgage payment for the farm. So, I started praying. I really thought we could make it, but this was a big step.

Night after night, I sat in the family room with tears, praying for clarity. I talked to some mentors and one of my old college professors. I even did some strategizing to make sure we could afford it. I couldn't get fixed on what God wanted me to do, but I was pretty sure He was leading me to work in the church but in a totally different way.

Trusting When We Can't See the Path

Two years earlier than anticipated, I walked into the office at the pharmaceutical company and turned in my resignation. Everyone thought I was crazy. To the outside world, it looked like I was walking out on a dream job. My boss wanted to give me a week to make sure I truly wanted to retire. And I'll admit, it was a bit frightful. It's hard to make such a big change after twenty-four years. I had an amazing career, and at forty-eight, I had plenty of time to

Searching

keep advancing. I had the life everyone wanted. I finally told him, "You can give me a weekend or a week. It doesn't matter. My mind is made up."

And just like that, I walked away from a career most people live for.

That weekend, I flew to Canada to go to a conference with my friend, Trevor, from Strategic Coach®. Suddenly, I was retired, and it was time for me to see exactly what God had prepared for me.

Trevor asked me a series of tough questions. He wanted to know where I saw myself in the next stages of my life, and he posed a list of questions from Strategic Coach and Dan Sullivan's D.O.S.® Conversation. One question hit me hard. In fact, it sort of offended me. But after I truly considered it, the reality brought me to tears. "Lamarr, do you know who you are? Apart from your corporate life, do you have an identity?"

I didn't have an answer.

Maybe King David felt the same. "Who am I?" he asked twice. The first time, even though he'd been proclaimed the next King of Israel, he hadn't embraced his potential. "Who am I to become the king's son-in-law?" Later, when God promised to establish David's throne forever, the King asked again, "Who am I . . . that you brought me this far?" David had spent so many years being the youngest son of Jesse, a shepherd, and then in hiding, it took him a while to grab hold of what God created him to be.

But that's like most of us. We get so caught up in what we've been doing that we allow our past to influence who we think we are—until someone like Trevor comes along and challenges us. Who am I?

Brenda thought I was crazy by now. Our lives got very intense for an extensive period of time, but I was determined to hold on to that piece of land I felt God had given us. I ran a consulting business and worked hard to make ends meet, but I'll be honest: it didn't look good.

I finally took a significant amount of my retirement and the savings we had planned to be able to live on through the rest of our lives and put it on the farm. I prayed and trusted that God would see our faithfulness and work in it. And although Brenda stood beside me and believed God for a miracle through it all, it took a toll on our marriage.

Winter at the Farm

In the winter of 2012, Brenda and I went away to celebrate our anniversary. We really needed the time away together, and the warm weather of an ocean cruise was a nice change from the temperatures in Chicago. For a few days, we had no worries, and the farm wasn't constantly taking me away from her.

On the way home from the airport, I pulled into the farm to check on the houses. As soon as I walked in, my heart dropped. Water dripped from everywhere and was ankle-deep in both places. I immediately called the plumber we had used for the church a number of times. While I waited, I went out to break the news to Brenda.

"It's what?!" Brenda just stared at me in disbelief.

"It's flooded. Everything is ruined."

I could see her thoughts. She was tired of dumping money into the property, and she was even more frustrated at how much time I spent there.

"Let me take you home, and then I'll come back to meet the plumber."

When I got home, I traded my cruising clothes for winter attire, then headed back to meet the plumber. We unsuccessfully searched for the water shut-off, and the plumber said, "It doesn't feel like the heat is on."

Searching

"No, it has to be. I made sure to set it at sixty-five before I left."

"I don't know, Lamarr. It feels pretty cold in here. Let's go check the meter."

We traipsed through the snow to the back of the house, and he pointed his flashlight toward the problem. "There's a lock on your meter, Lamarr."

"What? No way!"

"Did you pay the bill, man?"

"I know for sure the bill is all caught up. Why would they put a lock on the meter?"

"I don't know. But you'll have to get this straightened out before we fix the pipes."

When I got home, Brenda was waiting for me. Tired, I just wanted to go to bed, but she pointed out she'd spent more than twenty years supporting me while I worked long hours at my corporate job and with the farm, and now it was her turn to talk.

By the time she finished explaining her frustrations, I knew I needed to do something. She was correct. I had been absent too many times in our marriage while I traveled for business, and now I was letting the farm drain our retirement. I didn't know what it would cost to repair those houses, but I knew I needed God to take care of our marriage just as much as I needed him to take care of the houses.

The next day, I called the gas company. The first person assured me my bill was current and both the farmhouse and the coach house had service. After I convinced her they did not, she sent a repairman. A couple of other guys came to look at the damage, and a few execs tried to find the notices they said they sent me to tell me we needed to reconnect the gas after the utility company had replaced both meters. Finally, one of the vice presidents called me in for a meeting.

No one could find copies of those letters they supposedly sent. And while they refused to accept responsibility for the mess, they did attach a check to the envelope that contained the no-fault, no-contest agreement. But God had prepared me for this moment. Twenty-six years as a vice president responsible for minimizing liability gave me a huge insight into this man's motivation.

They'd gotten two bids on repairing the guesthouse and offered us a check for the amount of the larger estimate. All I had to do to get the money was sign the agreement.

"On the surface, your offer looks fair," I started. "But I know that estimates often fall short. What should I do if I need twenty-five percent more to finish the work?

"We thought the higher bid would be a solid way to a reasonable agreement."

"I appreciate your desire to do the right thing; however, I think it would be beneficial for us both if you gave us an open purchase order for the amount of this check plus fifty percent. If we need more than that, I'll come back to you. If we can get it repaired for less than the amount of your check, you'll come out ahead."

After asking a few questions that revealed my background and experience, he continued, "And you'll sign the agreement?"

"Yes, sir." I knew he just wanted that paperwork signed so the matter could be settled.

"I think we can make this work for both of us, Pastor."

When I got back home and told Brenda the story, she smiled. I wasn't forgiven, but she wasn't giving up on me.

"I guess I'm never going to be your hero."

"Oh, you're my hero, alright," she said. "But you keep flying around in that raggedy torn-up cape."

We Needed Another Miracle

Thanks to a miracle from the Lord, we completely renovated the farmhouse and guest house. But Brenda still wasn't convinced we should hang on to the farm. We went through a number of processes trying to figure out exactly what God wanted us to do, including trying to sell the property. We searched for God's will but just couldn't seem to find it.

Meanwhile, we received two offers on the property. The local village council squashed the first one immediately, so when the second was within days of being approved, we began to have some hope. I felt certain the village wouldn't pass up the opportunity for tax revenue. The developer wanted to build several high-end homes on the land.

As much as I loved the idea of having a church on these grounds, we really needed to get out from under this financial burden. We planned to set up a Chick-fil-A franchise, and the thought of running between the restaurant and the farm was taking its toll, too.

Brenda's feelings that the farm had a hold on us and wouldn't let go were confirmed when the developer called to tell me the deal we thought was a sure thing fell through. I didn't know how to tell her. The village council had denied their request. Not only did that kill that offer, but the property became impossible to sell to any kind of developer. The farm was not going to let go of us.

We eventually invited another couple to join us in a prayer walk. Brenda and I and this other couple just walked the property, praying that God would make it clear what we needed to do to honor Him with this farm.

That's when God helped us see we weren't supposed to tear down all the buildings and give him a modern sanctuary. He showed us that we were supposed to rehab the barn and the houses and turn the barn into a church.

I'm guessing David knew how I felt as I waited for God to give me clarity. Like David, what the Lord promised didn't happen overnight. David had the assurance he would be king, but I'll bet it was hard to keep that vision in mind while spending years hiding from Saul in caves. Psalm 57 gives us a clue to how he felt: "Have mercy on me, my God, have mercy on me, for in you I take refuge. I will take refuge in the shadow of your wings . . ."

I understand those kinds of cries. When we took over the farm mortgage, it kind of felt like that cave, and even after God gave me clarity about this property, God only gave me what I needed at the moment I needed it. For three years, we worked daily on rehabbing the barn and making it into something beautiful, but the path was very challenging. It would have been handy to know a week in advance how the Almighty had planned to take care of the landscaping, but he kept me guessing—and answered in ways I would never have imagined—right up until the last minute.

Transformation at the Barn

When we started transforming this barn, our church consisted of three or four families meeting together with $1200 in the bank. Though I'd followed God throughout my years at the pharmaceutical company, I realized I was sort of lost. I knew I needed to find my true identity, and even though I believed God wanted us to use the farm for something amazing, realistically, it looked a long way off.

Shortly after our prayer walk, we invited a contractor who specialized in church construction to come out and tell us how much it would take to get the barn ready for worship. We weren't thinking anything fancy, just enough to get in.

"Well, Lamarr, before you do any work on the barn, you're going to have to do some landscaping so you can get people in. By the time you get the parking lot and site work done and make a way into the barn, it's going to cost $350,000. So, I'd say to get everything inside and out finished, it will be a little over two million. What kind of budget do you have?"

"Right now, we have $1200 in the bank."

"What?!"

"We have about $1200 right now, and we're trusting God for the rest."

"You're kidding me, right?"

"No."

"Lamarr, I'm not sure what your plan is, but my company works with large churches across the United States. If that's all you have, we aren't going to be able to work with you. I'm sorry for the misunderstanding."

"Are you sure? You guys have been referred to us as the best in the business."

"We are, but if all you have is $1200, I just can't help you. I wish you well."

He walked toward his truck, and I called out after him. "Hey, when we finish this project, would it be alright if I call and invite you to our first service."

He laughed and said, "Yeah, you do that." And he left. He wasn't the first person unable to see the vision, and he wouldn't be the last. The saddest part of his disbelief is the many miracles he missed witnessing. Time after time, God showed up when we least expected it to help us carry out His vision. Fortunately, I had Dad and Madea's upbringing singing in my head. They had taught me never to give up and to believe all things were possible with God.

This farm that God gave us has transformed many lives, but none more than mine. I've stood in awe of God's plan at every turn. My Redeemer has brought multiple people into my life and allowed me to experience things I never imagined. Though I thought I understood the concept before,

I've learned more fully that when a vision is completely tied to Him, His will, and His purpose, there's no limit to what He can do.

Listening for Your Higher Calling

God taught me many amazing lessons during this uncertain time. Most of all, I discovered the power in reaching my higher calling. Look at how God worked in the lives of Joseph, Daniel, David, and Samuel—from slave to second-in-command, servant to satrap, shepherd to sovereign, and son to the seer of Israel—each of those men had no idea they had a calling so high we'd be talking about them millennia later. Had they limited themselves to a calling they could envision, the entire world might have died in a famine, or lions might have eaten Daniel. But these men understood these words from Oswald Chambers, "When we have the right relationship with God, life is full of spontaneous, joyful uncertainty and expectancy."

As you move forward to find your higher calling, take some time to read the history of these men that God prepared and used to do great things for Him. You'll find Joseph's story in Genesis 37-50, the recount of Samuel and David in 1 Samuel, and Daniel's encounter with God in the first six chapters of Daniel. Additionally, make a list of all the things you've gone through in your life, from the most insignificant to the most traumatic. Include every blessing and surprise. Then, think about all the things you learned along the way. It might be handy to create a timeline. Record the chores you had when you were eight, as well as your first job. List the extracurricular things you did at school, the instruments you played, and the clubs you participated in. As you journey through to find your higher calling, you will discover many of those events prepared you for the road you're on right now, and you might even see the direction God plans to take you.

God has more for us than we can imagine. He tells us, "My ways are higher than your ways, and my thoughts are higher than your thoughts" (Isaiah 55:9). And when we pursue that higher calling, we discover the adventure that Mr. Chambers described. I have a passion to help people uncover their higher calling, to realize the dream that will take them out of the land of mediocrity and into a grander vision. God wants to work in us things we can't do on our own.

In order to understand our higher calling, we must also answer the question, "Who am I?" And to do that, it is imperative we learn to listen. Proverbs 2 instructs us to make our ears attentive to wisdom and incline our hearts toward understanding. Solomon says this is the key to understanding God and His knowledge. Listening, or making your ears attentive, is the key to any great relationship, and your relationship with God is no exception. As our congregation walked through the barn-rehab season, God gave me a six-part strategy for the skill that uses LISTEN as an acronym: Learn, Inspire, Serve, Think, Encourage, and Navigate.

I can't wait to share all the ways God has been working in a little place in Libertyville, Illinois, and the huge transformations He accomplishes when folks LISTEN to Him when He calls their name and says, "Meet Me at the Barn."

PART TWO
Listen

2

Learn

We Should Only Stop Learning When We Stop Breathing

John Wesley once said, "The first priority of my life is to be holy, and the second goal of my life is to be a scholar." This man of God knew the value of being a lifelong learner. Samuel offers us a great example of the importance of learning. He was still a boy—maybe not as old as when I started depositing my parents' checks—when God spoke to Him for the first time. Three times, the Almighty called, but Samuel hadn't learned yet that God likes to communicate with His people. The Bible tells us, "The word of the Lord was rare." Samuel had to learn what the voice of the Lord sounded like. The priestly prophet lived to be very old, but he never stopped learning, nor did he quit listening.

Like a Child

Learning is a lifelong journey. Too many people think that after they've graduated, they're done—some stop before that. As an infant, every human searches for knowledge. Curiosity drives tiny people. They want to learn to roll over, talk, walk, and do the things their grown-up counterparts do. But somewhere in grade school, there's a shift.

A segment of children continues to thrive in the learning environment, but another part starts to dislike school—they get bored or feel like they aren't smart enough. Unfortunately, some of that comes from the adults in the children's lives. They hear phrases like, "I'm not good at math" or "I never liked science." Worse still are the kids who live in households where no one will help them learn. Whatever the origin, these children begin to wear the gown of negativity the adult wove for them, and they give up on learning.

Other children struggle with bookwork. If we could give them some hands-on work at a young age, they'd probably experience less discouragement. It's not that they don't want to learn; it's just that the subjects required in school don't interest them. Some of these folks will become mechanics, computer techs, or artists. All they need is an adult to help them understand not everything we need to learn can be taught in school. One of the greatest gifts you can give children is to help them find things that interest them so they can feed their need to learn.

Sadly, many adults consider learning a time of torture rather than an opportunity to grow and develop. These folks don't understand that lifelong learning makes the day-to-day an adventurous journey. When we begin to see every hurdle as an opportunity to expand our knowledge, learning becomes exciting.

A Journey Not a Destination

    Learning ultimately helps us answer that elusive *Who Am I?* By viewing every experience as a time to explore, we discover our interests and reveal our talents. When we see the learning process as a journey rather than a destination, we develop a better perspective. The journey allows me to become who I am and who I need to be. When learning is a destination—a college degree or a certificate to hang on the wall—we stop short of being able to walk in the freedom of who we were created to be.

    Consider the apostle Paul. One of his biggest problems while he lived as the Pharisee Saul was that he believed he had arrived. He had trained at the feet of the number one scholar at the time and thought he had nothing else to learn. So, when Jesus came along preaching a message that didn't line up with everything in the Talmud, Saul balked. His closed mind meant he couldn't learn anything from Jesus. He thought he knew it all. Without the ability to learn, he turned into the worst kind of bully and forced God to knock him down a peg or two to make him useful. So, blind and humbled, the great Saul had to be led by his hands into Damascus until a follower of Jesus Christ could rescue him and help him see—not only physically but mentally and spiritually.

    The closed-minded man who lived as the Hebrew Saul would never have considered using the Greek version of his name. On the other hand, after his encounter with Jesus, the apostle embraced his true identity. He took on the Gentile name of Paul so he could minister to the people he swore would never be part of the Kingdom of God. His meeting on the Damascus Road invited him to recognize the value of looking for lessons from God. Paul told the Corinthians to run the race in such a way as to win. He said, "I don't run aimlessly. I'm running so I won't be disqualified for the prize." The lifelong learner Paul understood that without the constant hunger to learn new things about how God works, his growth would be stifled. He vowed to keep running until the end. Only when he knew that Caesar was about to end his life did Paul tell Timothy, "I've fought the good fight. I've finished the race." Paul had taken the journey of learning and was heading for his destination—life forever with Christ.

Learning Means Unlearning

In the book *My Utmost for His Highest*, Oswald Chambers' wife shares this quote, "It is not true to say that God wants to teach us something in our trials. Through every cloud He brings our way, He wants us to unlearn something." As we set out to build a church, I had some unlearning to do. My corporate mindset saw a shiny new building in that field, but I had to unlearn the mindset that newer is better.

The Apostle Paul had the same challenge. He had learned that honoring God meant persecuting those whose actions didn't line up with what he believed to be righteous. Unfortunately, the teaching he adhered to contributed to his three days of blindness—a cloud that helped him unlearn many of the ideas he'd developed in his very formal teaching atmosphere.

People who've suffered abuse at the hand of their father might need to unlearn that all fathers, including their heavenly Father, are abusive. Many dads are wonderful, and our heavenly Father loves us in a larger capacity than we can comprehend. In fact, His example teaches us how to be a truly tremendous parent.

We need to unlearn prejudices and stereotypes. It's time to unlearn negativity—especially negative self-talk. By unlearning those things that divide and separate, we can learn to connect and love. Unlearning is a foundational part of our ability to learn.

Lessons from the Barn

The farm held a variety of lessons for me. I learned that Brenda and I had a stronger marriage than we knew. The stress of a $4000 monthly mortgage put a strain on our relationship; however, we've always kept God in the center, so we held on to Him until the storm passed.

I also learned about the cost of renovations. I had estimated the funds needed to get the property ready for worship at about $100,000. So, when that contractor told me it would be closer to $2,000,000, it seemed overwhelming. But when we found an architect to come on board with us, he confirmed that number. I had no idea where we would come up with that kind of money, but I trusted God to carry out His will.

God taught me tremendous lessons about how He works. For example, on the day I found out the second developer wouldn't be able to purchase the property, I went out to walk the grounds feeling lost and defeated. As I approached the first of the two houses, a white van pulled into the driveway, and a middle-aged woman dressed like a street vendor popped out.

I walked over to her van, and she introduced herself. It turned out that she stopped by just to visit the barn every time she was in town. I know it sounds odd, but she was a barn and landmark historian.

"I stop by every now and then to make sure the old girl is standing, and a developer hasn't come out to tear her down," she quipped.

I laughed, "No developer will be taking this barn down anytime soon. The village just took a wrecking ball to a deal I had with a developer."

"Oh good!" She paused a moment. "I don't mean to sound insensitive, but there aren't many beauties like her left."

The historian pulled a book from her van and showed me a photo of our farm from fifty years before. It looked like a Norman Rockwell painting. "This picture was taken back when this was all God's country," she said.

God's country—the phrase took me aback. "That's what this place was supposed to be," I told her. "I really felt like God was telling me to turn this barn into a church."

"Oh my! That would be perfect." She started talking fast and excitedly. "Lamarr, this is a rare barn. It could be a little goldmine. Thank God I stopped by! Now you have someone to help you."

"You know how to restore old barns?"

"Oh, I don't do the pounding and painting, but I know people who do. And if we can get historical preservation status—and I'm certain you can—well, there are a lot of people who love to help restore these old barns who will come to your aid."

"Wait, wait. I want to build a church, not a tourist location."

She laughed. "Only the outside becomes the tourist site. You can do anything you like on the inside. We just have to get your application filled out."

We chatted a bit more, and the barn expert promised to help us fulfill God's vision. Before she left, she handed me an autographed copy of her book and instilled some hope in my heart. When I broke the news to Brenda that the developer's deal had fallen through, I also told her about the barn lady. And we both learned a bit about God's timing.

Learning to Connect

After we discerned that God wanted us to renovate the barn, we started asking Him for a name for our new congregation. We wanted it to be a place where people of all races and ethnicities could worship together, and as we prayed, we decided on *Connection Church*. It would be a gathering where people could connect to Jesus and other believers.

As I said, our bank account boasted $1200 when we started clearing out the barn. But that truth didn't deter us; we decided we could begin with what we could do. So, we started spreading the word about *Connection Church* and our farm. We shared the vision and started cleaning out the barn. Armed with brooms, shovels, wheel barrels, and masks to keep out the smells and years of dust and dirt, we took over.

The lower level of the barn had nine horse stalls and a slab of concrete down the center. The upper level contained an enormous amount of dirt and even more holes. I'm pretty sure if four guys had all run into one of the walls at the same time, it would have come down. Brenda said we probably couldn't even get chickens to go to church in that barn, and she wasn't wrong. We found grain bins, an old sulky, and a few decomposed animals. Growing up in a small neighborhood near South Bend did not prepare me for all the things you'll find in a place where horses once lived.

As we cleaned the lower level, God reminded me of one of my boyhood mistakes. When I was about thirteen or fourteen, South Bend started a program called "Rent a Teen." They paired teens with people who needed help and were willing to pay for it. So, my friend and I signed up. We were excited when we got our first assignment. They gave us the address, and we got on our bikes and headed out. It was a long way from our houses, and when we arrived, we realized we'd been hired to work on a farm.

A very sweet lady came out to greet us. "It's so nice to meet you boys. I've got some work for you to do over here."

She took us into her barn and handed us each a shovel and a wheel barrel. "All you need to do is shovel all this and put it in the wheel barrels. When you get them full, you can take them way over there in the field." She pointed to a spot a good distance away. "Just keep shoveling and dumping until you get down to the concrete."

That didn't sound too hard. My friend and I had never been on a farm before, so we looked at it as an adventure. The nice lady went back into the house, and we got started. The summer day was pretty hot, but we didn't mind—until we had each put a few shovels worth of debris into the wheel barrels. The aroma began to teach us a lesson—this wasn't dirt.

After fifteen or twenty minutes, the owner returned. "It's a hot day. Would you boys like some fresh lemonade?" That sounded really good. So she headed back to the house to fix us something to drink.

We kept digging and digging, and finally, my friend said, "I don't think I'm gonna make it, Lamarr. Let's get going."

"No, come on. We're gonna get paid."

"Do you know what we're digging through here?"

"Yeah."

"I don't care how much she's payin' us. I don't think I can take this. Do you think we could take off while she's gettin' the lemonade?"

"What?!"

"We gotta get outta here, man. We're gonna be smellin' like this forever."

I did not want to smell like that, so we peeked out the door to see if she was coming back yet, and since the coast was clear, we took off.

Fast forward to 2013, and forty-eight-year-old Lamarr picked up a shovel in the lower level of that barn. As I filled that wheelbarrow with horse manure and dirt and the aroma began to rise, I learned God has a sense of humor. I guess it was time to finish that job I started thirty-five years earlier. It might have been a different barn in a different state, and the mask helped a little, but I still had to haul wheel barrels full of horse manure out into a field.

From Learning to Listening to Leading

If we want to be lifelong learners, one of the first things we have to do is find a mentor. And one of the best places to find a person to help us move toward Jesus is in a Christ-centered church. Paul set the example. After spending three years in Arabia with the Holy Spirit, he returned to Jerusalem and found Barnabas. The Encourager helped Paul answer the question, "Who am I?" Paul had unequivocally tied his existence to the Pharisees and being a persecutor of Christ's followers. The new apostle probably had a bit of an identity crisis after his experience on the Damascus Road. He truly had to make his ear attentive to wisdom in order to learn about the person he had been persecuting and define himself again.

After he had grown enough to share his victory, Paul himself took on young Christians to mentor. Timothy learned under Paul's watchful eye—so much so that the apostle called the young man his son. Paul mentored Titus, Onesimus, and countless others. He finally told the church at Philippi, "What you have learned and received and heard and seen in me, do; and the God of peace will be with you." (Philippians 4:9 RSV)

Take a minute and list the people God has put in your life since your childhood and the lessons they taught you. What have you seen and heard them do, and what parts of their lives should you imitate? Learning from people who follow God gives us a head start in finding our higher calling. We need to make certain the people we learn from and imitate look and act like Christ and want to help us do the same. These mentors will become for you like Trevor and Sam

Learn

Dalton were for me. They'll challenge you to learn the truth of who you are. And then, as Paul promised, the God of peace will be with you.

While we'll always want to learn from other Christians, we'll eventually grow to the point where our primary teacher will be Christ Himself. Jesus told His disciples, "Take my yoke upon you and learn from me, for I am gentle and humble in heart, and you will find rest for your souls. For my yoke is easy and my burden is light." (Matthew 11:29-30) It takes a bit of maturity and self-discipline to move from learning under the direction of a mentor to listening to Christ. But lifelong learners don't let that stop them.

Dig deeper into scripture. If you don't read the Word at all, start with a few verses a day. If you already read the Bible every day, grab a journal and begin writing the things God says to you as you read. Additionally, pray as if you expect God to speak. After telling us to make our ears attentive and turn our hearts toward understanding, Proverbs 2 goes on to explain that we should cry out for insight. In other words, we should long to learn. Our prayers show God our hearts. Crying out for insight demonstrates our passion to learn. As you pray, be sure to listen with your heart as you talk with Him and watch what happens around you because He often speaks through our situations.

Negative self-talk might try to tell you Jesus only talks to the pastor or the leaders in the church. Your past hurts might try to convince you God wouldn't talk directly to someone like you. But each of those mentors one day walked where you walk now. The only difference is they made a decision to never stop learning.

The yoke of learning can be cumbersome sometimes, but Jesus promised to take the bulk of the weight so it wouldn't be too heavy for us. If we want to develop the skill to LISTEN, learning from Jesus is vital.

After we've learned to hear Jesus speak and begun learning from Him, we can move into leading. Like Paul, we become the mentor. Jesus commissioned us: "Therefore go and make disciples of all nations, baptizing them in the name of the Father and of the Son and of the Holy Spirit, and teaching them to obey everything I have commanded you. And surely I am with you always, to the very end of the age." (Matthew 28:19-20) One of the best ways to continue learning is to teach others. Ask any Sunday School teacher or Bible Study leader. In fact, Corrie ten Boom said, "The best learning I had came from teaching." Anyone who has ever led a group will tell you that preparing to lead someone closer to Christ accelerates your own learning process. When you have to stay one step ahead of those you're leading, you dive deep into scripture and books. You'll find blogs and sermons and truly enjoy the treasures you find as God reveals truths to you to pass on to those He's entrusted to your care.

Learning is the first step in the LISTEN model. Without the willingness to learn, moving forward will be impossible. Learning helps us answer the question, "Who am I?" Knowledge gives us confidence, and with that confidence comes a greater sense of worth and identity. Fortunately, each of the letters in LISTEN offers us opportunities to learn. So, let's move ahead and explore the need to Inspire.

3

Inspire

It Takes a Team to Realize a Dream

If we truly want to LISTEN to God, we need to surround ourselves with inspiration. Everyone we come in contact with has a bit of influence over our lives. If we allow ourselves to be fed with negativity, we will have nothing but negativity to give. On the other hand, an inspiration-filled team will fill us with inspiration that we can pass along.

I feel blessed to have had so many individuals inspire me as we journeyed toward the completion of the barn. Too many people, especially as they move into positions of authority, try to walk through life alone. But we need others. In 2013, long before any work commenced on the barn, inspiration flowed from the basement of our home. Two young men who were interested in ministry joined me in laying out a three-year strategic plan. Our vision board contained all the things we wanted Connection Church to become. We envisioned a prayer ministry and bringing in the lost for the Lord. Demolishing racial and ethnic divides made the top of our list. So much of what we wrote on those boards became reality.

Whether you call them your board of directors, inner circle, or small fellowship group, you need people who understand what's important to you and can inspire you to become the best version of yourself. The best kind of inspirers share their ideas and listen carefully to yours. This group of trusted individuals should know your goals so they can help you stay focused. Plus, they have a vision. They've grabbed hold of what God has shown you and added to it with what God has shown them. Helen Kellar, though blind, understood the vital nature of a vision. She said, "The most pathetic person in the world is someone who has sight but has no vision." We need inspirational visionaries on our team.

The trials of everyday life easily distract us. Sometimes, we allow disappointments or setbacks to define our reality. It's easy to lose hope when everything looks dismal. The groups we choose to surround ourselves with need to be able to see past obstacles and keep God's vision in front of them. Everyone experiences doubt at times, and while we don't want people to feed us wishful thinking or the view from rose-colored glasses, we do need a team who will remind us of truths. The truth they share should come from scripture, prayer, and the vision we've received from God.

These will be the people you pray with—much like the couple that walked the property with Brenda and me before we realized the barn would become our worship center. Your inspiration team will also be willing to work with you.

The Connection Team

When work started on the barn, God brought us the perfect team. I had known Pastor Ken and his wife for decades. After helping start a couple of large churches, including one of the largest churches in Illinois, he'd been called to Tennessee to plant a congregation. After eight years, he completed his work in that area, so we asked him to be part of Connection Church. I felt God telling me Pastor Ken would be the perfect person to help us build a diverse congregation. Both of us had lamented the segregation in worship centers. What better way to encourage people of all races and ethnicities to worship with us than to have a black and a white pastor co-lead?

In addition to Pastor Ken, God added to the diversity by bringing a local Filipino pastor to us. He was getting ready to start a church in the area and wanted to walk through this vision with us so he could learn and help us.

In addition to our diverse leadership, an architect who knew what we needed to do to get the village to approve the inspections joined our team. He created a design so we could use the space to its fullest. As you might imagine, the barn lady became a member of our team even before we started building it. She just happened to be the president of The Barn Restoration Association of Illinois. When I asked her to be part of the church as well as the restoration team, she hesitated.

"I doubt your congregation will really want me. Most churches I've been to don't accept me. I've been divorced."

"That's not who we are. You really have to give us a shot."

The barn lady contacted some of the restoration experts she knew, and one of them became an additional member of our team. He was very encouraged by what we were doing to keep the barn and offered to help us in any way he could.

God had sent a team of experts. I had no idea about restoring a barn, but the Lord brought these people to add to the inspiration of this place of worship.

The Pivotal Part of our Team

As we worked, we prayed and believed God would send the right people to help build this church. One day while cleaning the main level of the barn, we found plywood lying on the floor. When we moved it, we discovered huge holes. The father-in-law of one of the guys who worked with us visited from Arkansas one weekend and volunteered to show us how to fill in the huge gaps so no one would fall through. Even my son learned how to work a saw while we cut boards to cover those holes.

After months of labor, we finally had the barn somewhat presentable. Several of us decided to hold church in there for just one Sunday. It was a long way from being complete, but we wanted to see what it would be like to have a service in the barn. We laid a rug on the floor and ran extension cords. I set up a projector, and we planned to hold our first worship service.

A few days before that first service, an older gentleman stopped in because he had heard about what we were doing. A friend of his had recommended he drop by. He and I talked for almost two hours. I discovered his name was Mike, and he was a master carpenter. He was about sixty-one at the time and had learned the skill from his dad when he was twelve. Mike had served as the lead carpenter building some of the largest churches in our area.

After we talked, I said, "Mike, I believe God brought you here to help us." He protested a bit, but I continued. "You're a carpenter, you've built more churches than anyone I know, and we've been praying God would send someone."

"I don't know if I'd say God sent me."

"I'll tell you what, we're going to meet here in the barn on Sunday. You see what God tells you."

That next Sunday, Mike came back.

He said, "All right, I'm going to show you how to do this."

Mike came back every Sunday for the next three years.

I have more to tell you about Mike, but for now, I'll just share that his skills and participation in our team felt like a bit of inspiration directly from God. Mike's expertise and encouragement were just what our church needed to move forward. He became a pivotal part of our team and our congregation.

Inspirational Teams from the Bible

Moses was one of those people who found himself being prepared for a larger role at a very young age. His experience made him kind of a loner. Left in a basket as a baby and raised in the palace as part of the royal family–but not really—he learned how to fend for himself. Then, when he defended one of his fellow countrymen, everyone turned on him—the Egyptians and the Hebrews. For the next forty years, he had only himself and his wife, and only Aaron and Joshua made his inner circle when they headed toward the Red Sea.

But Moses' story demonstrates how desperately a leader needs a team. As he led the people through the wilderness, the stress started getting to him. He barely had time to sleep. Fortunately, Moses took his father-in-law's advice. While in his eighties, he selected one man from each tribe to be his inspirational team and seventy more to lead the hundreds of thousands of Israelites. In his book *Good to Great,* Jim Collins said, "Great vision without great people is irrelevant." Since even a man with direct access to God needed an inner circle to be everything God created Him to be, we should assume we need one, too.

Though Jesus had heaven inspiring His every step, He left us a tremendous example of our need to build a team of individuals to walk with us. Jesus chose twelve men to join His team—three He made part of His inner circle. These men journeyed with Christ and then split up to take His message throughout Judah.

The Bible tells us Jesus often took them into remote places so He could meet with them alone. Yes, He taught them and prepared them to carry on after He returned to heaven; however, they helped Him stay fed and brought people to Him whom they thought he could heal.

Jesus also showed us that we might choose a person who isn't very inspirational every now and then, and even the most inspirational might abandon us from time to time. Jesus had to deal with Judas. And the other eleven scattered right when He needed them most.

What to Do When Your Team Abandons You

As you may have guessed by now, the team from Connection Church wasn't my first group of inspiring friends. When we purchased the property, Brenda and I were part of a good-sized congregation full of supportive God-followers. As I said, I was one of several guarantors on the loan.

When the disciples left Jesus alone with the soldiers, they were running for their lives. Fear drove them. They felt as though they didn't have a choice. In much the same way, the men and women who left the church didn't have other alternatives. They had to find employment and take care of their families. The lead pastor who left had to follow God's higher calling. Not one of them intentionally abandoned me; however, I felt alone for a while. When the financial aspect of their choices tried to pull Brenda and me apart, their desertion took a toll. It would have been easy to have given up on building a team or allowing people in. That's a typical response. Humans don't like to be hurt.

Jesus set the example. He immediately began fellowshipping with those eleven guys after His resurrection. Despite Judas' betrayal, Peter's denial, and the other ten leaving Him high and dry, Jesus rebuilt His team and continued inspiring them.

Following God's plan will get overly scary at times, and some folks just can't handle it. But all that means we need to be even more determined to surround ourselves with inspiration. We can't allow the feeling of being discarded to keep us from taking the chance on the next team God brings to us.

There's also a good chance we will choose the wrong people—people who don't see God's vision or those who intentionally sabotage our efforts. Still, we can't let that possibility keep us from trusting.

The Non-Inspirational Choice

Joshua learned to follow God by imitating Moses. By the time he took over as leader of the Israelites, he had grown into a great man of God. Joshua led Israel into victory after victory. The surrounding nations grew fearful of the Israelites with the new leader at the helm. But even the greatest leaders make mistakes.

When the Gibeonites heard how powerful the Israelites had grown, they came to trick Joshua and make a treaty. The men of Gibeon came across as honest, respectable guys. Their offer seemed reasonable. So, Joshua didn't go to prayer before he made the deal. Let me just say it didn't end in a very inspirational way.

At the beginning of the project, Mike helped me take care of most of the things a general contractor would do. After working together for a while, he recommended a friend he'd worked with before to take over the project. I met his friend, and we decided he fit the bill. He had the credentials and the desire, so it seemed reasonable. Reasonable—that's what got Joshua into trouble.

For a long time, everything ran smoothly. But, about two-thirds into the rehab, things seemed to slow down. Then, when the time came to put the double doors in the main entrance, the general contractor kept putting it off. This entrance was critical in obtaining our occupancy permit, so I kept after him. Each time I asked about it, he had another excuse.

Finally, I felt like the general contractor wasn't being honest with me, so I started doing my homework. I found out he hadn't paid all the contractors, and though I tried hard not to think the worst, I started to wonder where he had found the money to buy the new sportscar he had started driving six weeks before. Although he had taken the most recent draw from the loan, even Mike hadn't been paid. So, I finally had to confront the guy.

He said, "No, no, Lamarr. I've been paying for everything. That door is just not ready yet."

"Really? Because Mike said he hasn't been paid in four weeks."

"Uh, well, I just got a little behind."

"I need you to get Mike paid this week. Mike's a part of our church. He's been here every day helping us, and we already gave you the money to pay him."

He got Mike caught up, but two weeks later, we found ourselves back in the same situation—Mike with no paycheck, vendors with outstanding invoices, and the vital doors still nowhere to be found. So, I confronted him one more time. This time, Mike was in the room.

"This is our third discussion about the doors. Where are they?" I asked.

"I think we need to measure one more time to make sure we get the right size."

"What are you talking about? We already gave you the money, and you said you ordered them and put the deposit on them."

"Well, no. I didn't get them ordered."

"You know what? You have no more credibility with me. I'm done. I feel like you've been taking some of the funds we paid you, and I'm not going to let God's money be used like this anymore. Today's your last day. Take your stuff. I need you to leave."

"You're gonna do me like that?!"

I said, "Just pack up your stuff, put it in your truck, and leave."

He said, "Well, if I'm done, I'm taking Mike with me. Come on, Mike."

Mike and this guy had been friends for thirty years. I'd only been his pastor for a year. Mike looked at me, then his friend. He had a decision to make—one that could greatly impact the future of our project. I wasn't sure where I'd find someone to replace his talent.

Mike was such a humble guy. I'd never seen him stand up to this friend. In fact, I'd watched the general contractor take advantage of Mike more than once. But this friend had always been Mike's boss, and Mike had always done whatever his friend told him.

Mike finally looked at him with tears in his eyes and said, "I'm not going anywhere. My place is here."

We all stood there for a moment. "It's time for you to leave," I told Mike's friend. I was proud of Mike for standing up to him. I knew it was really hard for him.

The guy mumbled under his breath the whole time he packed up his truck. When he left, his tires threw dirt and gravel all over the place. He was angry, and I took on the position of general contractor.

We like to blame the devil for getting in the way of God's goodness, but disobedience is a much more likely source. The enemy doesn't have to come around if we refuse to act Godly. Unfortunately, even when we follow God faithfully, we're directly affected by the people we surround ourselves with.

We took the first suggestion for a general contractor, but sometimes I wonder if God wanted that job. I don't like to be presumptuous when it comes to what God does and why He does it, but after that contractor left, we began to experience additional blessings. Our Savior started to send gifts that were essential to the project.

When we do Kingdom work, we will face opposition. The Romans and the Sanhedrin both came against Jesus. Still, He never gave up. Jesus understood that Kingdom work always comes with great personal cost and pain. Jesus kept the disciples close to inspire Him, and although we never want to put our trust in humans, we need that type of inspiration.

While we have to be careful when putting together our inspirational team, it's important to accept the chance you'll get a Judas or less than honest general contractor. It will be tempting to go it alone to avoid the possibility, but we need a team. This kind of group is significant to our growth and carrying out our vision. Without their influence, we risk becoming complacent or settling for the status quo.

Yes, you might let someone in who ends up being uninspiring, but you'll be in good company. Our church did it, Joshua had his moment, and even more convincingly, Jesus risked it. If you want to be able to truly LISTEN, you'll need a team. So, be in prayer, asking God to send you the people you need in your life to accomplish His purpose and give you the freedom to become everything He created you to be.

The Greatest Source of Inspiration

Scripture will always be our greatest source of inspiration. Those sixty-six books offer countless verses to lift us up and point us in the right direction. Proverbs 2 tells us to "seek [wisdom] like silver and search for it like a hidden treasure." The easiest place to seek wisdom and inspiration is within the pages of God's Word. For instance, when the nation of Israel was about to be sent into exile, God asked Jeremiah to pass a message to them, and it's still inspiring millions of people today: "For I know the plans I have for you," declares the Lord, "plans to prosper you and not to harm you, plans to give you hope and a future" (Jeremiah 29:11).

Often, we have a difficult time embracing the fact that God wants to prosper us. But if we want to be able to take full advantage of the inspiration around us, we need to believe God has a plan—a perfect and wonderful plan. He sees our future, and He wants us to hope in Him.

Paul sent the people in Rome a letter full of inspiration. He told them, "And we know that in all things God works for the good of those who love him, who have been called according to his purpose." (Romans 8:28)

Fear is the enemy of inspiration. When we hold onto apprehension, we can't hear those who try to inspire us. Romans 8:28 has the power to combat anxiety. When fear tries to talk us out of what we're certain God has called us to do, we have the assurance that even if we get it wrong, God can work it for good. Our responsibility is to simply love Him. This reduces the pressure and can help us forge ahead when worry and trepidation try to trip us up.

Plus, Jesus wants to carry all our troubles. His greatest desire is to remove all your inspiration killers. Peter tells us, "Cast all your anxiety on him because he cares for you" (1 Peter 5:7). We usually use the word cast as a fishing term. When we cast a line, we throw the bait as far into the middle of the lake as possible. That's what God asks us to do with our cares. He wants us to toss those difficulties as far from us as we can. Jesus cares about us. He doesn't want us to focus on those negative moments.

Before you can move forward, you'll need to build your inspiration team. Create a list of those you already have in your inner circle. Make a careful and prayerful inventory. Do each of them bring inspiration to the table? Do they assist you in "making your ear attentive to wisdom"? If you don't already have this crucial component to your vision, write down all those who might be a good fit. Pray over that list and contact them. You will need help on this journey, and a team of inspirational Christ followers can help you carry the load.

Next, make a list of your inspiration killers—your doubts and fears and the people who speak negativity into your vision. It's time to cast these into the middle of the lake. Paul told Timothy that Jesus doesn't give us a spirit of fear. (2 Timothy 1:7) So, take those fears to God and cast them His way.

Christ came to inspire us. He sends friends, family, mentors, and teachers to give us inspiration and help us answer the question, "Who am I?" Because when we are inspired, we begin to embrace the fact that with God, all things are possible, and we're able to truly LISTEN.

4

Serve

Service Gives Life and Refines Your Vision

Jesus emphasized the importance of service. He told His disciples they should serve God, but even more often, he told them to serve each other. He made sure they knew even He didn't come to be served but to serve (Matthew 20:28). He said the greatest should become the least, and the leader the one who serves (Luke 22:26). It's a concept that turned the disciple's thinking upside down, and it creates the same kind of disturbance today.

In our acronym, the S stands for serve—an action that always turns attention toward someone or something else. In a world where selfies, self-realization, and self-sufficiency have become commonplace, few want to think about serving. Oh, they'll help others in a third-world country or take care of the homeless, but what do you think about serving the person sitting next to you in a restaurant or the team member who reports to you at work?

In his book *Purpose Driven Life*, Rick Warren reminds us, "The only way you can serve God is by serving other people." And in serving God, we begin to hear Him more clearly. Service becomes pivotal in discovering who I truly am.

Serving at the Barn

I can't overstate the significance of service in bringing the barn to life. Although I get credit for writing this book, and I lead the congregation that meets on the farm, the story of the barn has never really been about me. Every drop of sweat and millisecond of time was an act of service performed to create a place where people from everywhere can come to be served while they learn about Jesus' love. We then help them understand the beauty of serving the Lord and others.

If it weren't for the multitude of folks who came out to sweep, shovel, and carry debris, it would have taken six months longer to complete the first phase of the barn. Many of us completed tasks we'd never done before. For instance, my son played sports and had a great high school academic career, but he discovered he had the ability to use a saw when we started filling those holes in the floor.

Mike was the picture of service. Not only did he never miss a Sunday, but he also touched every aspect of the barn. In addition to introducing us to the general contractor, Mike brought his friend Gabe out to help. The two of them implemented every design I requested. Near the end of the build, I envisioned a fireplace in the children's ministry area. Mike drew up the plan and created it. I have a photo of Gabe and Mike on two ladders hanging the sheeting on the outside of the barn. I love sharing that picture and telling people Michael and Gabriel completed the bulk of the work.

Service gives us an opportunity to find out who God created us to be. It can often be key in uncovering the answer to "Who am I?" Supporting others through serving molds us and helps us explore the different positions in ministry so we can find the area God has saved for us. When you serve while you are learning and inspiring, it can become an outpouring of both, particularly if those around you view you at a higher level in life than they are.

When Jesus washed the feet of His disciples, it spoke volumes. Their Master and Teacher took on the role of the lowliest household servant. He showed them no one is above serving. The same thing happens when we give of ourselves to those who feel as though they're worthless. The impact we have on when we serve is endless.

Service Means Being Willing to Get Dirty

Mike and I developed a tremendous relationship while building the barn together. We enjoyed coffee together every morning and more than a few late dinners. For two years, he recalibrated much of my thinking. But it wasn't always smooth sailing. We experienced setbacks, delays, unexpected expenses, and even faced some disagreements.

Serving reminds me of all the times Jesus used the vineyard as a metaphor for working in the kingdom. Since so few of us ever work in a grape field, we don't understand how dirty the farmers get. The vines get sharp when you prune them, so there's a good chance you'll get some cuts. Plus, they need plenty of water, which means carrying bucket after bucket or digging trenches to create an irrigation system. The grapes themselves stain your hands as you harvest them, and the hard work causes sweat.

We hear about Peter's protest when Jesus washed his feet, but we seldom consider the dirt he encountered on those sandal-clad feet walking sandy and dirty roads every day. We read right past the part where John tells us, "Jesus laid aside His robe." Why did He do that? Probably because washing feet has the potential to make you dirty.

Getting dirty as you serve is just as impactful as giving yourself to those who feel insignificant. Realizing a person is willing to risk filth to act on your behalf sends a message bigger than most words can carry.

The barn offered a variety of ways to get dirty. Even before we built our team, the people from the church came out every weekend to help haul wheel barrels full of dirt, manure, and debris out of the barn. These people donned masks to avoid the smell and dust, and we all worked together to power wash, sweep, tear down the horse stalls, and more. They removed horse stalls and used sledgehammers to break up all the concrete in the lower level.

Outside the barn was just as dirty. We had to cut down trees, clear brush, drain stagnant water, and remove an underground colony of bees. Yes, dirty sometimes meant a little dangerous, too. I got stung twice, but that wasn't nearly as bad as Mike's service injury.

I arrived at the barn one day to find Gabe running toward my car.

"Lamarr, follow me, Mike's hurt bad."

Our master carpenter sounded disgusted with himself when we found him. "Thirty-five years at this, and I've never done anything so careless." When he saw me, he addressed Gabe, "You didn't have to go bother Lamarr over this little cut."

Mike's little cut had already bled through the rag they'd wrapped around it. After a bit of a disagreement about our opposing definitions of "little cut," he finally agreed to let me take him to the hospital. There, we discovered he'd already netted himself a blood infection. He protested a bit about being admitted but stayed five full days until they were sure the infection was gone.

Dirt and injury are risks we face when we serve. Service isn't always pretty or glamorous, but God promised that those who put themselves last will one day be first, and service is the perfect way to put yourself at the end of the line.

There Are No Excuses in Serving

Mike and I met at the barn every morning at 7:00 a.m. and worked thirteen or fourteen hours each day. It didn't matter how long we'd worked the day before or how late we'd gotten to bed; we never missed our early morning appointment.

Excuses just don't cut it when you're working in Christ's vineyard. Many of our team had blisters and tired muscles, yet they showed up day after day. A Baptist church from Michigan visited us a couple of times just to work. They could have found any number of reasons to stay home. Still, they made the trip twice to help us create a space where people of every race and ethnicity could have the freedom to be who God created them to be.

Moses may have been the chief excuse-maker. Imagine this leader of Israel standing there in front of that fiery bush that wouldn't burn up. Despite the miracle right before his eyes, he comes up with several excuses. "Who am I to go talk to Pharoah?" I'm thinking he's the perfect guy. He's the only Israelite to have lived in the palace. But God was gracious. Even though he had some issues with our core question—who am I?—God simply told him, "It's OK, I'll be with you."

This brought Moses to excuse number two. "What if the Israelites don't want to follow me? I think I need to know your name." Again, the ever-forgiving God told Him, "I Am Who I Am. Tell them I Am sent you."

In order to convince Moses he didn't need to worry, God then tells him all the plans He has to help him get the people out of Egypt. The Almighty showed Moses two miracles in addition to the bush and the fact he could hear God speaking out loud to him. Still, Moses kept going with the excuses. "I don't speak well." After this, it sounds like God may have been getting a little weary of hearing Moses' complaints. I don't know whether Israel's leader didn't hear the irritation in God's voice or just ignored it, but he finished his list of reasons he shouldn't go by speaking the truth. "Lord, please just send someone else." Scripture tells us God's anger burned against Moses. Nevertheless, Moses was still the person God chose to take His message to Pharaoh, and He gave Moses the gift of a helper and a mouthpiece—Aaron.

Like Moses, we may be tempted to say, "I've never done that," or "I don't think I can." Fortunately, service makes for a great training ground. When an opportunity arises to serve in a way that sounds inviting but you aren't positive that it's God's call, volunteer on a short-term basis. Try the new thing for ninety days. You may discover it's something you have been preparing for all your life. Yes, it might be scary, but we can't let fear stop us.

Fear Is Not a Reason to Avoid Serving

Moses was afraid. You can't really blame him. He left because the palace guard wanted to kill him for breaking up a fight between an Egyptian and an Israelite and killed the Egyptian in the process. After living with him for forty years, Moses knew Pharaoh better than most. He'd probably had a taste of his hard heart before he left for Midian.

But God didn't accept fear as a reason for not serving. Fear is False Evidence Appearing Real. Moses didn't tell God anything that wasn't true in Moses' mind; however, there was a bigger truth that negated the reality Moses had created in his brain. God was going with him, he had the power of The Great I Am to go with him, and the Creator knew his limitations as well as his abilities. Charles Stanley said, "Basically, there are two paths you can walk: faith or fear. It's impossible to simultaneously trust God and not trust God." So, much like Joshua said, "Choose this day whom you will serve," we must choose for ourselves what we will fear.

Fear tried to stop me and Brenda. The farm seemed to be coming between us, and it looked like it would drain our finances beyond what we could withstand. Charles Spurgeon said, "We are foolish to expect to serve God without opposition: the more zealous we are, the more sure are we to be assailed." Serving God doesn't mean everything will go perfectly. It does mean that when we go where God calls, He has everything under control. And God had His hand on that farm. It would not sell, no matter how perfect the deal looked. We didn't realize it then, but God had a bigger truth we hadn't seen yet.

When fear tries to keep us from serving, we have to look for the bigger truth. Embracing Moses' story and the tale of our barn as truth can help you move past the fear. Whenever we feel fear trying to quash our vision, we need to search for God's truth. The obstacles right in front of us can seem so real. In fact, if we share them with a human who doesn't look for God's point of view, that person will confirm the false evidence. Moses' false evidence made sense to any rational human. No one would have blamed Brenda and me if we had given in to the false evidence that stared us in the face.

Fortunately, God sent those inspirational people to show us the bigger truth. Moses had Aaron. Brenda and I had the barn lady, Mike, and those who prayed the perimeter of the property with us. When we begin to see God's truth, the lies that appear real fade, and with it, the fear that keeps us from serving.

Serving Involves Sacrifice

The longer I worked with Mike, the more I realized his claim of being a master carpenter was an understatement. He could have worked anywhere and named his price. His knowledge, commitment to excellence, and work ethic were without equal. Still, he chose to accept our meager pay to bring God's vision to fruition.

More sacrifice came from that Baptist church from Michigan. They gave up precious time to drive two-and-a-half hours to labor with us as we cleaned. They were excited to see us make the barn into a church. Their sacrifice inspired us to keep going and continue to pursue God's vision.

One of the reasons sacrifice is crucial to service is that it means we begin to let go of the things we're holding on to. Even letting go of excuses and fear can be a sacrifice to people who have allowed those things to become part of their identity.

Brenda and I had to let go of the security of the pharmaceutical company as well as our savings. We had to let go of doubt and our own plans. Some will give up pride. Missionaries who travel overseas for months and years at a time let go of their families.

Elisha gives us a tremendous example of sacrificial service. He was plowing the field when Elijah invited the younger prophet to join him in his travels. But before he would go, Elisha asked the older man if he could return home and tell his family goodbye. While there, he slaughtered the oxen he was using and burned his plow. Elisha didn't simply let go of his past. He put it so far behind him that he eliminated his reasons to go back.

Sacrifice is never easy, but it's key to freeing us to be everything we were created to be. Those things we hold on to—the lies that look like they'll keep us safe or bring us joy—are really holding onto us. We often think that sacrifice is about what we give others. However, like service, sacrifice has the potential to add quality to our lives as well.

Serving takes us one step closer to truly being able to LISTEN. It changes our perspective, and we begin to understand ourselves better as we also grow and start to experience the freedom to be who God created us to be. Serving opens the door to imagining amazing possibilities.

Biblical Service

Joshua led the people of Israel faithfully through many years. He knew his death was near, but he also knew that humans get distracted easily. So, he challenged the people. "But if serving the Lord seems undesirable to you, then choose for yourselves this day whom you will serve, whether the gods your ancestors served beyond the Euphrates or the gods of the Amorites, in whose land you are living. But as for me and my household, we will serve the Lord." (Joshua 24:15)

The Israelites had a history of picking up other gods. Joshua understood that following God and serving Him was an intentional choice. The world will knock us down again and again. Sometimes, God's plan feels unclear. When those times come, doubt becomes fear's companion. If we haven't made a conscious decision to serve God, we're more likely to succumb to the False Evidence.

Joshua may have also given this mandate because he knew service keeps us focused. When we serve Christ, it helps us keep our eyes on Him.

Serve

Ephesians 6:7-8 says, "Serve wholeheartedly, as if you were serving the Lord, not people, because you know that the Lord will reward each one for whatever good they do, whether they are slave or free." Mike was the epitome of serving wholeheartedly. He didn't complain when the general contractor stopped paying him, and although he nearly severed his hand, he wanted to keep working. That's because Mike didn't focus on the things the world thought were important; his heart's desire was serving God to make Connection Church a place where people of every cultural background could come together to find freedom to be who they were created to be.

Plus, although the motive for serving can never be the reward, it's exciting to know the Lord has wonderful things waiting for those who serve as if they were serving Him. Rewards come in the form of new relationships, financial blessings, seeing God work in miraculous ways, and, ultimately, a place in Heaven.

Paul reminded the Galatians to avoid getting caught up in the benefits. "You, my brothers and sisters, were called to be free. But do not use your freedom to indulge the flesh; rather, serve one another humbly in love" (Galatians 5:13). Freedom is a gift to those who call Jesus their Savior. Salvation means we obey out of love rather than an attempt to follow a list of rules. We no longer live under the pressure to be righteous because we're clothed with Jesus' righteousness. It's easy to become arrogant in our newfound freedom. Several famous Christ followers have gotten caught up in their own righteousness, forgetting it was a gift from God.

That's why Paul told the people in Galatia to serve one another. Service keeps us humble. It reminds us who we are and how we got here.

When you begin to consider ways you can serve, your first order of business will be to put Joshua 24:15 into action and make an intentional decision to serve God. Then, if you really want to make it a wholehearted effort, pull out that list you made at the beginning of the book. Pray over each item. Look for ways things on that list might fit in your church or community. Make a list of jobs—paid and volunteer—that God might have been preparing you for. Even if someone else is doing those things now, let someone know you're interested. Don't wait to be asked. Mike and the barn lady would have missed so much if they hadn't stopped by.

Service gives us even more opportunities to learn and inspire. It's one of the best ways to answer the question, "Who am I?" and it opens the door to new and adventurous possibilities.

5

Think

Impossible Is Not in God's Dictionary

It's easy to focus on the impossibilities. No one older than five has trouble seeing what can go wrong. And when we start looking at the negative, that fear we talked about creeps back in—False Evidence Appearing Real.

Fear took some of those families out of the original church, and the seeming reality of our congregation raising two million dollars brought laughs from the first contractor we called. Fortunately, for those who believe in following God in His vision, the possibilities are endless. I even had some moments of doubt before we got started, but God kept pushing me forward.

We often sell ourselves short by not consistently thinking about possibilities that exist for us as an individual. While I worked for the pharmaceutical company, I obsessed over the question, "What if I could retire from corporate America by age fifty." And then I started thinking, what if I could retire sooner? I turned my thoughts toward possibilities. And then I began to wonder, *What journey or path do I need to proceed on to make sure I'm ready for that possibility?* That thought process helped me accomplish what many thought impossible. I retired from corporate America after only twenty-four years. Thinking about the possibilities created a big, audacious goal at an early age. The sooner we turn our thoughts to possible rather than impossible, the further we can go on this journey and the faster we can get there.

This is the concept that brings us to the T in LISTEN—Think. It's vital to turn our thinking toward what can be if we want to live in the freedom of all Christ created us to be.

Thinking about the Possibilities

As we focus our thoughts on the possibilities, we have to ask ourselves, "What do we truly desire? If money were no object and we had all the time in the world, what would we like to see happen?" So often, we allow funds and scheduling to be a catalyst for FEAR. Life will throw enough obstacles in our path; it's imperative we don't allow our thoughts to become boulders that stand in our way.

Psalm 37:4 says, "Delight yourself in the Lord, and He will give you the desires of your heart." Few understand that when we focus on Christ, He puts desires within us. Some actually try to suppress their desires because they feel selfish. But if you're seeking Jesus, it's important to think about those desires as God-given possibilities. We need to give ourselves permission to transform our thinking. Rather than looking at our desires as silly dreams or selfish fantasies, those who delight themselves in Christ can see their desires as visions from the Lord.

D. L. Moody said, "If God is your partner, make your plans big!" Too many times, we keep our thinking small. If a thought crosses our mind that seems outrageous, we dismiss it. Instead, I challenge you to ask yourself, "Is that thought too outrageous for God?" The T in LISTEN may be the most difficult hurdle to leap because it involves transforming our thinking. Fortunately, if we've made up our minds to be lifelong learners and surrounded ourselves with an inspiring team, it will be a bit easier to rid our brains of limiting beliefs.

After we open the door to believing all things are possible with God, we begin to ask, "How committed am I to achieving that goal?" Many give up way too easily, but it's usually because they haven't committed to the vision. Not long ago, I talked with a couple about where they saw themselves in the future. We talked about their current level of happiness and where they would like that to be. When I asked the question, "What do you desire?" They had to really think about it. When they finally had an answer, I said, "OK, let's write that down." Next, I had them look at their desires in print and consider the question, "How committed are you to this destination?" Our commitment to the destination reveals the depth of our desire.

When the journey becomes rough, we need that vision and a reminder of our commitment to help us keep going. Though the desires and visions look impossible for humans, we have the God of the impossible on our side.

Funding the Impossible

I've already told you that I truly thought the entire renovation would cost somewhere in the neighborhood of $100,000; however, after investing that amount—primarily from my own funds—we were still a long way from using the space as a worship center. The floors and walls were clean, but the light coming in between the boards reminded us the structure needed some stability and insulation. We couldn't keep going without more money.

So, I drew up a business plan. Every financial institution I showed it to saw only the apparent reality. Between what we owed on our home and the mortgage on the farm, loaning us the rest of the two million made no sense from the world's point of view. I had one other idea.

A few years prior, I had been a part of the board for Converge MidAmerica, a Christian body that invested seed capital in churches. I was highly aware of their investment criteria, and I knew the barn didn't fit their portfolio philosophy. But that wasn't the only thing that made Converge seem like an unlikely investor. I worried the size of the loan we needed would look like a conflict of interest since I was one of them. But I needed a miracle, so I put aside my hesitations. After all, what did I have to lose?

The first hurdle was getting a spot on the board's agenda. They created that list prior to the meeting, and it was relatively set in stone. Regardless, when I showed up at my final meeting, I took one of the board members aside and pled my case.

"Can I have fifteen minutes with the committee?" I told him a little bit about the barn.

"You know how this works, Lamarr. We have an agenda, and getting anything on it after it's been set doesn't happen. This is a big ask. We can't afford the perception that we're favoring a board member."

"I'm not asking for a check. I just want to share my dream, my vision of faith. Tell them I just want to address the board to give them a final farewell, tell them where God was leading, and share my gratitude for letting me serve for fifteen years."

He hesitated for a moment but agreed to ask.

After we finished the hugs and greetings, I plugged my laptop in and told them how much I appreciated being able to serve with them over the years. Then I said, "I just wanted to show you where God's taking me next. A picture's worth a thousand words," I said. I turned on the presentation and planned to spend the next ten minutes showing them the progression photos of the barn.

My fifteen-minute time slot quickly expanded. Every time I gave a short description of a photo, question after question ensued. Finally, I knew I'd run over my allotted time. "Hey guys, thanks so much for allowing me to share. I've always enjoyed working with you, but I think I've exhausted my fifteen minutes."

The head of the board spoke up. "Wait, before you go, how much will it take to finish it?"

"About $1.2 million."

"Well, thanks for coming, Lamarr. We really appreciate your service over the last decade and a half." He stood to shake my hand. "Would you mind hanging out in the hall for a few minutes?"

The next thirty minutes felt like an eternity as I paced the corridor. When they called me back in, the head of the board motioned me to take the presenter's seat and asked me to close in prayer. Now, I was totally confused, and my face must have shown it.

The board chair smiled. "Make sure it's a prayer of thanksgiving because you've just secured the money to finish the barn."

"What did you say?" I stammered a bit.

"We've decided to loan your church the money to finish your Higher Calling initiative. Now, let's pray."

And pray I did. I'm not sure what I said to God other than I was tremendously grateful, and I'm confident it was not the most eloquent prayer I've prayed. The shock overwhelmed me, but not as much as the thankfulness.

God of the Impossible

Matthew 19:26 says, "With man this is impossible, but with God all things are possible." In Philippians 4:13, Paul said with confidence, "I can do all things through Christ who gives me strength." We need to stand on these verses if we want to keep thinking about all the possibilities. It's easy to give up when whatever we're doing gets hard or looks hopeless, but if we're working on God's vision, the words can't and impossible don't exist.

Granted, we can't run ahead with our own vision and expect God to jump through our hoops. On the other hand, when journeying with Jesus, doors open—sometimes at the last moment—and regardless of what we think the timing should be, His is always perfect.

God let Connection Church do something with Convergence we would never have been able to do with a conventional lender. Setting your own payment amount and interest rate falls in the category of impossible. Still, that's exactly what God allowed us to do. We requested a payment and rate we could afford in the present with terms that increased over the years, so it was equitable for the lender in the long term. And the impossible became possible.

Too often, humans allow their thinking to limit them, and with those limitations, they shut God out. The Bible tells us Jesus did few miracles in Nazareth because they lacked faith. (Matthew 13:58) Imagine Christ back in his hometown. He knew everyone. I'm sure he wanted to heal His childhood friend's mother and provide for the people He grew up with. But their belief put limitations on the Almighty, and He honored their thinking. What if the obstacles in our way are the same thing—God simply honoring our thoughts?

Too Big for Our Britches

Pride often gets in the way of thinking about the possibilities. If we're not careful, we start to make plans that fit inside our capabilities. We're not good at asking for help. It requires a humbling that most don't want to submit to.

In addition to finding that support team for inspiration and asking them to assist us, we must be willing to lay ourselves bare in front of God. Perhaps one of the reasons Adam and Eve were able to commune with God so intimately is that they were naked in the Garden, yet they felt no shame (Genesis 2:25). They allowed themselves to be completely vulnerable before their maker, and with their vulnerability came a perfect relationship.

On more than one occasion, I had to reveal my whole heart to God. I resorted to tears and crying out because the situation looked dire. When Brenda and I were struggling in our marriage, I surrendered our union wholly to the Master of relationships. In the days when bankruptcy threatened, my cries reached the One who holds the riches of the universe in the palm of His hand.

Even kneeling in prayer falls into the category of humility. God really doesn't give much credence to our posture when we pray—stand, sit, kneel, walk, fall prostrate; He doesn't care. However, the position of our hearts is of utmost importance to Him. Even those who can't kneel because their limbs won't let them can bow their hearts before God. For many, physically kneeling in prayer is difficult, not because they need a knee replacement, but because the posture signals a release of pride not everyone can handle.

Crying out holds the same significance. People who cling to the impossible are often incapable of pouring their hearts out to God. Pride imprisons them. It won't allow them to fall to their knees or put their face to the ground. Uncontrollable tears demonstrate vulnerability.

Billy Graham said, "When we come to the end of ourselves, we come to the beginning of God." Crying out is more than your typical prayer. The undignified nature forces us to embrace humility, and it allows us to come into the presence of God. Pride can't see the Creator.

The farm cut into my pride on more than one occasion. Like Peter, I had to step onto uncertain waters, knowing I could never keep my head above the surface on my own. When I hired Mike, I didn't have the money to pay him. The church's bank account fluctuated between zero and twelve hundred dollars for years but never rose above that.

Hiring Mike and cleaning the barn with no promise we could finish was an act of humility. The entire congregation kept their minds focused on the possibilities. We had to completely lean on God and trust He had a way to carry out His plan. Otherwise, we would have given up long before we realized we needed more than a million dollars—we didn't even have hope of getting the one hundred thousand I thought we needed.

Take the Next Step and Let God Work

What looked impossible to outsiders became more and more real as time went by. As Mike and the general contractor began to explain to me the scope of work that needed to be done to make the barn structurally sound, my mind's eye grabbed hold of it. The more information they gave me, the higher the price tag. At the same time, every description allowed me to think about the possibilities.

Meet Me at the Barn

When Michael and Gabriel climbed the ladders to put one of the layers of wrap on the outside of the barn to keep the wind from whistling through the holes, my only thought was of the angels God had sent to bring about His vision. The holes closing began to allow those walls we'd power washed to glow in a golden hue. And when one of the young couples from the church, Andy and Jen, asked to be married in the barn long before it could be finished, I knew others were beginning to think about what was possible.

Obstacles abounded when Andy and Jen asked about moving their wedding to the barn. But I told them I would pray about it. After a discussion with God about where He wanted this wedding to take place, I knew I needed to have a talk with Mike and Gabe.

If Andy and Jen moved their wedding, we would have six weeks to get the barn ready. When I approached the carpenters with the idea, they thought I was joking. The floor wasn't ready, and the entrance needed work. If it rained, we'd need umbrellas and something to clean up all the mud. Plus, there was the little issue of no electricity. The possible was difficult to see.

Andy and Jen knew all these facts, but they viewed them as False Evidence Appearing as Reality. They'd been part of the rehab since the beginning and had put so much sweat and tears into this barn. But bigger than that, this young couple saw the possibility. They didn't even mind the prospect of calling every single wedding guest to tell them about the change of venue. Gabe couldn't believe it when even Mike jumped on board.

Six weeks later, the makeshift sanctuary was breathtaking. White cloth covered the bales of hay where guests would sit. When Jen stood under the wedding arch in her white gown, she looked like something truly holy. I've officiated at weddings since; however, none comes remotely close to the beauty and majesty of that one. Even Gabe was in awe.

The wedding became a pivotal point in the church's history. Joy overflowed for those families, bringing hope to the rest of the congregation. Though still in the early stages of rehab, even more people began thinking about the possibilities. God had a divine purpose for this farm, and the congregation who owned it felt as though they had a part to play in the orchestration of the heavenly Father's mighty vision.

Biblical Thinking

One big problem for humans is the distraction of everything around us. Like Peter attempting to walk on the water, we let the raging storm control our thinking. That's why the words Paul shared with the Colossians are terribly important. "Set your minds on things above, not on earthly things" (Colossians 3:2). Each time the world tries to show us things to FEAR, it's our responsibility to take our minds back to Jesus. When focusing on things above becomes difficult, praise will often transport us there. By turning our thoughts to praise, especially when the worries of life start to distract us, our minds can more clearly see the possibilities. Earthly thinking clouds Godly visions. It robs us of seeing our own potential as well as what God wants to do through us. On the other hand, when we fix our minds on things above, the obstacles melt, and we feel unstoppable.

One way to fix your mind on things above is to watch for ways Christ is working. Use a journal, and each evening, record at least three ways you saw God move. It might be as simple as a single flower that brightened your day or as big as our loan from Convergence.

Additionally, throughout the day, say a prayer of thanks when you know Jesus was with you. When God saves the raindrops until the moment you enter a building, praise Him. If the argument you expected was easily diffused, thank Him.

Peter told the followers of Christ the importance of staying vigilant as well as the significance of keeping your mind unobstructed by outside influence. He tells us, "Therefore, with minds that are alert and fully sober, set your hope on the grace to be brought to you when Jesus Christ is revealed at his coming" (1 Peter 1:13).

Life gets tough. If Brenda and I hadn't stayed focused on the goodness of God, our marriage may not have survived. And when it feels like we can't go on any longer, remembering the promise of our future at the end of the ages can help us remain hopeful.

This principle of thinking about the possibilities can be summed up in Romans 12:2. "Do not conform to the pattern of this world but be transformed by the renewing of your mind. Then you will be able to test and approve what God's will is—his good, pleasing and perfect will."

Neuroscientists have discovered that God's instructions in Romans align with the principle of neuroplasticity. The nearly one hundred billion neurons in your mind send messages to each other. Each positive thought rewires the synapse until your brain is literally transformed. Our job is to feed those neurons positivity and truth. If we keep telling ourselves something is impossible, we can't know what God's perfect and pleasing will is because God works in the realm of the humanly impossible.

Daily exercises like writing down praises and filling our minds with scripture, inspiring songs, books, podcasts, and blogs will feed those neurons. Not only that but the more we speak about endless possibilities to others, the more we can help retrain their brain, too.

Think

By transforming our thinking, we open the door to a new world. Embracing the fact that nothing is impossible with God and allowing that fact to renew our minds becomes a pivotal step in the LISTEN model. The T moves us into a position to test and approve God's will. We gain perspective, freedom, and faith—key components of people who become encouragers.

6

Encourage

Encouragement Creates Strength for the Encourager as Well as the Encouraged

I once heard a preacher tell a story about a general's final speech to his troops before they went into battle. Every man knew the possibility existed that several might not return. He said, "Men, I want to encourage you. But let me tell you what encouragement is. True encouragement is prompted by love, directed at fear, and gives a transfer of strength. Though I'm your commanding officer, I love every one of you and appreciate the commitment you have made to our country. I admire what you're prepared to do. So, these words to you are prompted by love."

He continued, "I also understand that the majority of you have never faced battle or been forced to put your life on the line, so this love I share is directed at the fear in your heart right now. I believe in you. Now, I want you to look at these three stars on my shoulder. I have the authority, leadership, and experience of a general, and I'm transferring that to you. I want you to go out in my strength and my experience as a general. My encouragement to you is prompted by love directed at fear, and I want this transfer of strength to encourage you to be the best you can be."

I've used that story many times through the years to remind me how to be an encourager and who I should bring into my circle of inspiration. We need to surround ourselves with people who love us, understand our fears, and are in a position to transfer their strength to us.

Encouraged by People Who Love Us

My parents and siblings taught me the foundation of encouragement shown through love. They pushed me to be the best I could be and believed I could do things other kids my age wouldn't have dreamed of doing. Encouragement shown through love means watching life stretch the people you care about and resisting the urge to hold them back, even when it involves them going into battle.

Every time I drove onto the farm property during those years, I felt encouraged. Even after we hired professionals, members of the church kept coming to do the labor jobs. They saved us money and time by giving of themselves. Their love of Christ, other members, and people they hadn't even met yet prompted them to serve by getting dirty.

The beautiful thing about encouragement through love is that many times, you won't even recognize you're being an encourager. Those who came out daily or weekly to pick up a broom or haul away debris didn't do it to encourage me; however, that was the result. Our presence is a powerful thing.

When you sit with someone in a hospital waiting room or make a point to ask how a new job is going, you become an encourager. George MacDonald said, "If, instead of a gem or even a flower, we could cast the gift of a lovely thought into the heart of a friend, that would be giving as the angels give." Encouragement through love might be the easiest job we have.

Some of the most important encouragement we give will be to the ones we love. We have the power to shape our children, nieces, nephews, and the young ones in our churches. Kids today hear so much negativity. But every word of encouragement we share helps to counteract those negative words and thoughts. We can't control what others say or do to the children we love, but we can balance the scale with positivity and help build those encouraging neuroreceptors.

And while it's more natural to encourage children, the adults we encounter probably need even more encouragement. So many people have experienced abuse and abandonment. They have trained their brains to weigh every statement through the lens of manipulation and negativity. Some hide it well. Others come across as mean or withdrawn. We have the power to change lives with encouraging actions and words. Even a positive text message or a Post-it™ note left on the corner of a desk can change someone's outlook.

When life gets rough, it's often easy to blame those closest to us. Our spouse or best friend can become the object of our frustration. That's when it becomes even more important to find ways to provide encouragement regardless of how we feel. Encouragement needs to be an intentional action rather than an afterthought or gut reaction. During those times when it's most difficult to speak words of encouragement, hugs, small gestures, gifts, and smiles can be effective.

Encouragement Directed at Fear

At the very beginning, when the original organization purchased the farm, we had a plan. The step-by-step destruction and construction proposal allowed us to have confidence in our ability to transform this piece of property into a beautiful church campus. We thought we had sought God's will, but I wonder if we'd really only seen the first leg of the journey and He hadn't revealed yet what lay around the bend.

When humanity's Plan B kicked in—which may have been God's Plan A all along—it came with some fearful moments. We had the desertion stage, the financial crisis stage, the strain on the marriage stage, and the find funding stage—and those were just the major hurdles. Fear tried to send us into a deep hole and drive a wedge between me and my lovely bride. And it nearly succeeded once or twice. However, Brenda and I chose to lean on God through the False Evidence Appearing Real.

We didn't anticipate the impact our putting the project into God's hands would have on others. Despite the threat of constant uncertainty, we held on to God and each other. My congregation and my friends knew I didn't have answers. They understood the financial strain of the decisions we had to make. Brenda and I never tried to whitewash the truth. Everyone saw what was going on, and they heard the same answer every time they asked the question, "How are you going to . . . ?"

"I don't know, but we serve an awesome God, and He will provide."

My attitude toward fear brought encouragement to everyone in my circle. It's not that I wasn't afraid. Believe me, if you'd heard my prayers and seen my tears, you'd know I experienced discouragement. However, I know love is greater than fear. I knew God loved me too much to let me down.

My church family and friends kept loving me through every moment, and when all that love became directed at fear, encouragement flowed.

Additionally, encouragement requires truth—real truth, not the False Evidence Appearing Real. When the question arose about how we could accomplish something, we didn't make up some false reality. We stated the truth. Sometimes, that meant an unknown was involved. Regardless, I could reassure everyone that God had everything under control. The truth about who God is and what He does is encouraging to those who trust Him.

The word encourage literally means to put courage into someone. No wonder it combats fear so excellently. Courage is not the lack of fear. Courage is perseverance in the face of fear. And when we push through because of love, we encourage others.

Mike remained one of our main sources of encouragement throughout the entire process. When we had problems with the general contractor, Mike didn't miss a beat. Though he had allowed that guy to berate him and tell him what to do throughout the project, he had mustered the courage to tell him they weren't a team. As that guy walked out the door, Mike said, "I guess I'm going to have to figure out a way to get those doors." The tension in the air automatically dissipated, and our project was back on track as though nothing happened. Encouragement directed at fear spreads like wildfire.

Encouragement Transfers Strength

When you encourage someone with your words or actions, you transfer strength to them. Some do it by leading, others by following. Regardless of your position, you carry this power.

Encourage

As Brenda and I talked and planned, we knew we were going to need some things for the church. As I mentioned before, Pastor Ken and I had been friends and ministered together for years. When he moved to Tennessee, Brenda and his wife kept in touch. So, when she found out the church Ken had started was closing, she mentioned it to me.

"Didn't you say we needed some musical equipment for the church?"

"Yeah, I've been looking on Craigslist for some drums."

"Why don't you call Ken and see if his church would sell us some of their stuff."

After a little back and forth about whether or not it was presumptuous of me to swoop in and ask for their stuff before they were closed, I called.

Ken was interested in helping. "What do you need, Lamarr?"

"Well, if you have some drums and extra chairs, that would be great."

"How much do you have in your budget for the musical stuff?"

"We have about $5,000."

"I have to check with the Elder board. Let me call you back."

Ken called back just a couple of hours later. Several board members had been in the church for a finance meeting, so he'd been able to talk to them about my request. After he explained, a strange voice came over the phone.

"Hey, Pastor Lamarr, we have you on speakerphone. It sounds like you're doing some exciting work over there. How can we help you?"

Then Ken's voice came on. "They want to know what you need."

"Pastor Ken, we need everything." I laughed. "Literally everything."

The first voice spoke again, "Well, as always, God has great timing. We were just discussing what we were going to do with all the assets. We wondered if you'd like to come and take all our musical equipment and anything else you think you'll need."

"I don't think we could afford more than the drums."

"No, we want to give it all to you for $5,000."

I was stunned.

A few weeks later, Brenda and I flew to Tennessee, rented a U-Haul, and drove to Pastor Ken's church. When Ken saw the size of the truck we brought, he laughed.

"Lamarr, there's no way everything's going to fit in there. You'll need to get the biggest U-Haul they rent to get all this stuff."

He took us inside and showed us what they wanted to give us—chairs, office equipment, drums, speakers, a mixer, tables, and more.

"You can have as much as you can fit in the truck, so you better go get a bigger one."

Brenda and I exchanged U-Hauls, and the next day, after the congregation heard our story and saw photos of the transformation of the barn, we started loading. Nearly every person in the church stayed to help. By the time we were done, we couldn't fit one more thing in that trailer. I can't begin to tell you how much money they saved us when they transferred their strength to us. But I can share that their gift encouraged us more than anyone might imagine.

Not all transfers of strength will be quite so tangible. Nevertheless, when we encourage others by showing them love directed at fear, our strength becomes their strength. When you can't go on any longer, encouragement will lift and carry you. And when we are able to share our strength with others, we are blessed in return. As John Greenleaf Whittier put it: "I'll lift you, and you lift me, and we'll both ascend together."

Encouragement Comes In Many Forms

We purchased the property in 2007 but didn't start renovations until the middle of 2013. The financial crisis began just a year after the initial purchase. So, for five years, Brenda and I felt beat up. We tried to keep discouragement at bay, but I have to admit that feeling overwhelmed us some days. The Lord's kindness encouraged us as we journeyed through the rehabilitation process. Person after person came out of what seemed like nowhere and became an integral part of the project. Even Pastor Ken and his wife moved near us after their church in Tennessee closed because he wanted to help.

As we neared the end of the project, our finances began to dwindle. Every time I checked the balance, I knew we'd be running tight to finish. That's when the village council and the county came out to let us know we needed to put in excess of three hundred trees and shrubs around the perimeter to separate our property from the neighbors on both sides and the back. Without these residential requirements fulfilled, we couldn't get the occupancy permit. And Mike pointed out that the size of the trees they wanted us to plant meant that even if someone donated all the trees, we didn't have equipment big enough to set them in the holes. A landscaping architect drew up plans that met the village's specifications and gave us an estimate. This project would cost close to one hundred fifty thousand dollars.

We didn't have that kind of money left. But that night, God gave me some encouragement. Brenda and I were attending Converge's annual banquet. As I was leaving, a guy with a familiar face stopped me. Though I couldn't place him, he knew about our church. After he jogged my memory, he asked how the barn was coming. So, I shared the news we'd received that day.

He said, "Pastor, do you remember what I do?"

"No," I said, "I'm sorry, I don't."

"Pastor Lamarr, I own a landscaping company. Maybe I could come over and take a look at it."

This landscaping owner's name was Rigo. He visited the next day to evaluate our needs, and while he was there, he shared his story.

He and his wife were suffering from depression. Their fifteen-year-old son had been killed in a car accident eighteen months earlier. Rigo, Jr. and a friend were changing a tire on an exit ramp. A car getting off the highway didn't see them, and Rigo's son had been killed instantly. The couple hadn't been the same since.

"One of the reasons I was really interested in seeing what you were doing over here," the landscaper told me, "is because Rigo, Jr. used to be the drummer at our church. He had begged me and his mother to let him be the drummer for a church about an hour from us, but we wanted him in church with us, and we didn't think it was good for him to be driving that far after he got his license. We had just decided to allow him when the car hit him."

After we walked the property and talked, Rigo shared again, "Pastor Lamarr, I really feel like God wants me to help you with this in memory of Rigo, Jr. If you can purchase all the trees and shrubs the village and county say you need, my team and I will bring our equipment and do all the work."

Not only did Rigo and his team serve the Lord by planting all those trees and getting the landscaping done around the church, but they also encouraged us as our funds got low. We wouldn't have been able to finish if Rigo hadn't helped.

Most of the time, serving will encourage us as much as it does those we serve. I believe this was especially true for Rigo.

Encourage

On his last day of landscaping, Rigo, Mike, and I stood near the front of the ground level of the barn. "What are you going to do here?" he asked, pointing to the ground under us.

"We'll probably put some blacktop here as the basic entry and walkway."

"Oh, no, Pastor Lark. You need pavers here."

"That would be awesome." Mike chimed in.

"We don't have money for that, Rigo." I hated to squash their plan. "We still have too many code requirements to finish on the inside."

"No worries about the money. I will do . . ."

"No, Rigo. You've already been way too generous. I can't ask you to give any more."

"I'm not doing this for you, Pastor Lark. This is for *mi 'hijo.*"

Mike began reminding me that this was an answer to prayer as Rigo continued. "Pavers will last a long time. I want to be able to come to this place and remember my Rigo. He loved the Lord so much. I will build a patio and stairway from here to the front door, so every time I come, I will know I did something for my son."

The three of us bowed our heads and prayed a prayer of thanksgiving.

Rigo took care of all our problems with the village and a few we didn't even know we had. He made enhancements we hadn't dreamed of nor could have afforded without him. The pavers looked marvelous, but as much as Rigo's gifts encouraged Connection Church, his giving, hard work, and our chats were an encouragement to him. He walked with a bit more resolve and the knowledge he'd done something pleasing for the Lord and us, which helped him with his grief.

Often times when we're in Rigo's situation, we don't feel like we can be an encourager. Plus, when we meet people who seem to be full of joy without a care in the world, we mistakenly assume they don't need any encouragement. I try to stay positive and thankful in every circumstance, so many might see me and think I don't need a pick-me-up. Every person in the world, regardless of their current situation, requires encouragement. A simple smile or holding a door open could be just what that joyful person needs to keep their tank full. Your words and actions make a much bigger difference than you might ever know.

The Ultimate Encourager

Scripture is filled with encouragement—reminders that God loves us and will never leave nor forsake us. Joseph sat in prison for years. He must have wondered if God had forgotten him until the Lord reminded him he had the ability to interpret dreams and later lifted him to the position of second-in-command. David felt tremendously vulnerable as Saul and the army of Israel chased him throughout Judah; however, he hung on to the encouragement Samuel had given him when the prophet anointed him to be the next king.

These two stories and others like them can be an encouragement to us if we let them. Proverbs 2 brings great encouragement. When we make our ears attentive, incline our hearts toward God, cry out for understanding, and seek wisdom like treasure, God promises we will find His knowledge. Verses six through eight tell us, "For the Lord gives wisdom; from his mouth comes knowledge and understanding; he stores up sound wisdom for the upright; he is a shield to those who walk in integrity, guarding the paths of justice and preserving the way of his saints."

Wouldn't you love to have the wisdom of the Lord? The Bible promises we can. On top of that, when we LISTEN for His wisdom, God vows to be our shield and guard.

Encourage

Reading and embracing God's word is vital to maintaining courage when False Evidence tries to convince us the things that Appear Real around us are winning. Joshua's story is filled with encouragement, too. The people of God won battle after battle because they trusted God. Joshua told them, "Have I not commanded you? Be strong and courageous. Do not be afraid; do not be discouraged, for the Lord your God will be with you wherever you go" (Joshua 1:9). Their enemies wanted them to be discouraged. Joshua challenged them to turn their "discourage" into "His courage." The promise of God going with us wherever we go should fill us with courage.

Isaiah 40:31 tells us, "Those who hope in the Lord will renew their strength. They will soar on wings like eagles; they will run and not grow weary, they will walk and not be faint." Encouragement is a by-product of hope. Like hope, encouragement allows us to soar and run. It keeps us from growing weary and faint. And the more hope and encouragement we have, the more we can pass along.

After sitting in prisons, being shipwrecked, and facing stonings, Paul knew the power of encouragement. "Therefore encourage one another and build each other up, just as in fact you are doing" (1 Thessalonians 5:11). Though he sent letters of encouragement at least fifteen times, he often spoke of how the care his friends administered brought him hope and courage.

One of the goals of the barns is to bring God's encouragement to everyone who enters or hears our story. Connection Church has felt the impact of our Savior's encouragement through all the miracles and blessings He's given us. Because of His kindness, we have a passion to pass that encouragement on to others.

You can pass along encouragement, too. Fill yourself with God's Word so you can remain courageous and then begin to share your stories. Tell people what God has done for you. Practice encouragement by mentoring someone or speaking words of kindness each day. Because as you encourage others, you will find yourself encouraged.

7

Navigate

Step Out Boldly and Join Christ in the Faith Journey

I love to talk to people. No matter where I go, people seem to open up to me, and as I listen, I've found many seem lost with no clear path. Few people understand their purpose. The world offers so many possibilities that pull us in a myriad of directions. Advertising aims to convince us we're missing out on something. Unfortunately, when we use that kind of thinking as a starting point to understand why we're here, we just find ourselves more lost. That's why keeping our thoughts focused on God's possibilities is so vital.

One of the reasons I invite people to Meet Me at the Barn is to help them embrace this LISTEN model so that when they reach the N, they can better Navigate life.

Each person has a unique path. The goal of Connection Church is to help individuals navigate the journey created specifically for them. Too many try to follow a path carved out for someone else. They see a friend or mentor walking in the liberty God created them to enjoy and think they can find joy by walking a similar way. But that's not how it works. When we learn to navigate our personal path, we can become the absolute best version of ourselves and begin to walk in the freedom of becoming everything we were created to be.

We call this part Navigate because practicing the LISTEN model is not about getting to the end. Listening means learning to enjoy the path as you move toward the destination—your goals, aspirations, and, finally, eternal life with Jesus Christ.

A GPS for Your Life

The story of the barn is a story of navigating life. Each step of the barn rehab represents a point in our life journey. People will abandon us. God will inspire us. We'll go through rough times when it feels like everything is falling apart. The Lord will use it to teach us a lesson. We'll make bad choices and try to work things out ourselves. Jesus will show us grand possibilities. We might even find ourselves cleaning up emotional manure and spiritual dead animals. Learning to LISTEN doesn't mean we won't encounter trouble. Rather, it gives us the ability to move through the difficulties in the most efficient way possible. Max Lucado summed it up nicely, "God never said that the journey would be easy, but He did say that the arrival would be worthwhile."

Teens today can't imagine using a map or printing directions from an online mapping service. They tell their phone the name or address of their destination, and a computer-generated voice instructs them which way to turn in five hundred feet. Twenty-first-century living means no one navigates across the country without their global positioning system.

The way the current phone GPS apps can detect slow traffic and accidents amazes me. When the satellite sees trouble ahead, it warns us and helps us navigate around it. The detours are sometimes cumbersome, but they get us to our destination with the fewest possible snafus.

LISTEN works similarly. It can't prevent the world from crashing, but it can help us navigate through or around the mess depending on what God knows will help us grow and push us toward our best selves. Plus, when we walk on God's route instead of our own, we uncover blessings. Everything we need will be provided—many times just when we need it. Unfortunately, we often try to take shortcuts or create routes through the fields—paths God doesn't carve out—in an attempt to retrieve those needs earlier than God intended.

Waiting on God can be very difficult. Sometimes, he lets us sit in traffic because the pause is still the fastest path toward our best selves. Worse than going through the field to get our needs ahead of God's timing—we think our wants are needs, and when we chase these distractions, we lose our way. We have no idea where our global position might be.

I unearthed some valuable lessons as we rehabbed that barn. I learned so much about myself as well as how to do things I never imagined. Looking for inspiration became a high priority, and my team discovered the folly of neglecting prayer when we're bringing someone into leadership. Our entire congregation began to think about and see the possibilities. And every time God came through, they had more confidence He would come through the next time, that in itself encouraged us to keep going.

That is how LISTEN helps us navigate our next steps. The more we learn, receive inspiration, serve, think about the possibilities, and encourage one another, the easier it becomes to see which path to take.

People often misquote Matthew 7:14 when they talk about staying on the straight and narrow. This translation has its roots in the King James Version, but it actually says, "strait and narrow." And in case you missed it in geography class, a strait is anything but straight. In fact, straits twist and turn, they have rocks and rapids because they are narrow waterways. Straits aren't always easy to navigate.

That's why we need a GPS, and nothing tells us our current position better than the Word of God as we learn to LISTEN. The Bible reveals the truth about who and whose we are. So many feel lost and can't answer the "Who am I?" question because they don't understand they are created in the image of God. They don't realize they have an inheritance prepared for them by their Father in Heaven. We find clear directions on how to live the best life possible in those pages—not rules or limitations, but a guidance system.

Following a GPS Takes Courage

Today, we've become so accustomed to allowing our phone to guide us from place to place that we don't question it. But consider the folks who used those first Magellans in the late 1980s. At the time, humans were so dependent on paper maps. Most cars had glove compartments filled with a plethora of meticulously folded navigational systems. Those first electronic GPS devices were only as accurate as the number of satellites you could pick up at the time, and a bar on the side of the screen provided this vital information. When you traveled through a less populated area, through a tunnel, or into a densely forested region, the signal would drop, and you had no idea when it would come back. A backup map was a must in the early 1990s.

LISTEN doesn't provide a backup map. We have to depend on the GPS—God's Positioning System—and sometimes the signal isn't as clear as we would like because we walk away from the origin. It takes courageous Christianity to walk toward the purpose God has for you.

I've learned that following God's Positioning System means I refuse to allow fear to paralyze me and keep me locked in my current situation. I have come to understand that fear will always be there. But as I hone my skills in LISTENing, I grow in the knowledge that fear has no power to stop me as I move forward.

Adjustments Along the Route

Every journey has a starting point. Let's face it: if that kiosk at the mall didn't say "You Are Here," we wouldn't know which way to turn to get to where we want. The LISTEN model allows us to see where we currently stand. But in order to move forward, we have to want to be someplace different. Without a hunger for a change of scenery, we'll be stuck in our current spot forever.

As we begin to navigate, the desire we discover as we think about the possibilities should steer us toward what we learn and how we think. Even the way we serve can help send us in the direction of our desire. The LISTEN Model helps refine our vision. The more we learn, the more clarity we have. We move and adjust when we realize we're a bit off course. These adjustments continually transform the way we think and open even more possibilities. As we serve, we discover talents we didn't know we had. Lifelong learners begin to realize they weren't created for some of the things they thought they would enjoy.

By honing your skills, you can hear the Lord speak. LISTENing is of utmost importance if you want to reach your higher calling. It unlocks success in your life. This means prioritizing who you allow to speak into your life. We must choose encouragers and those who inspire us to be part of our inner circle.

It's also significant to remember that listening does not mean agreement. I can listen to someone in my closest circle without automatically accepting and acting on their words. Take my daughters, for instance. When they were teenagers, they would ask for permission to go somewhere or buy something. They explained their rationale and waited for my response. However, if I said no or disagreed with their opinion, they voiced their typical complaint. "Dad, you're not listening to me."

Unfortunately for them, they confused listening and agreeing. The two aren't interchangeable. "I heard everything you said," I would tell them, "I don't agree with you, and I'm not giving you permission to go." Sometimes, I had to explain that the fact I had listened so carefully was the reason I said no. So, while listening is absolutely vital, it does not constitute agreement.

Even when we don't agree, we can learn. Madea hammered a listening principle into my head. She said, "Lamarr, God gave you two ears and one mouth for a reason. You ought to do twice as much listening as you do talking." Listening allows us to see other perspectives and forces us to clarify what we believe. When we disagree, we have to look inside ourselves and find out why we think the way we do. The answer solidifies our beliefs or adjusts them a bit as we hear another's thoughts.

Navigating Like King David

King David gives us a great example of using the LISTEN model to learn to navigate. He learned in the sheepfold as well as in the throne room. As the youngest of ten, David would have been able to watch his brothers and sisters as they grew. He saw his brothers go to war against the Philistines and had tremendous responsibility at a very young age.

Samuel presented David with a vision for his life before he turned thirteen. He knew he would someday be king. However, like our experience at the barn, David's vision didn't come to fruition overnight. He didn't take the throne until his thirtieth year. As we navigate, it's crucial to remember that so we don't get disheartened or distracted as we wait.

David lived a life of service. He served his family and King Saul. Even when he became a leader, he served his men and then his country and each act of service navigated him closer to his vision. The lessons he learned and the respect he gained as he served made all the difference.

As David hit adulthood, King Saul started showing signs of jealousy. The young king-elect began hiding out in the caves of Judah; however, he didn't escape alone. David surrounded himself with inspirational men and their families. These men believed in the vision Samuel gave to David and supported him during the most difficult time of his life. David's years in the wilderness remind us that even when we're following God's vision, there will be difficult times. Some think the road to God's destination should be smooth and easy, but that's seldom the case. That's why bringing inspirational people into your troubles is imperative.

David thought about the possibilities constantly. He found creative ways to hide and recognized God's provision every time Saul nearly discovered his whereabouts. The Psalms give us insights into David's desires and dreams. In Psalm 7, he cried out to God to save him. In Psalm 51, he was so distraught about sinning that his deepest desire was to have his sins forgiven.

Many of David's inspirational team became his encouragers. Several of them risked their lives to get water for him, and his inner circle exhorted him when he almost allowed his grief for Jonathan to squash the excitement over their victories. One of his closest confidantes was a prophet of the Lord. Nathan called him out when he stole Bathsheba from Uriah.

Those same men walked with him as he navigated life. He embarked on his journey when Samuel gave him the vision. He used that prophecy to shape his decisions and tell him which path to take. Learning to protect the flock taught him which direction to take to protect his team. Thinking about the possibilities gave him the courage to endure the trying years while he ran from Saul. He inspired and encouraged as he went because he surrounded himself with those who fed into him; becoming king was never his destination. The throne was merely a mile marker on his journey. Serving God as a man with the heart of the Lord every day helped him navigate through to his death.

Learning to Navigate at the Barn

When we learn to LISTEN properly, God not only provides navigation for us, but He also navigates others our way when He knows we need help. As I mentioned before, when the general contractor left, God started giving us little blessings. For instance, God navigated a member of the former church to us. This man stepped in and fixed a part of the floor we'd be waiting on the general contractor to take care of. But one of His bigger navigational moments was a gift we never expected.

A construction project down the road had ordered and paid for too much gravel. So, God navigated the dump truck onto our property. They had noticed the work we were doing on the barn and stopped and asked if we could use it. Of course, I said, "Yes, that will be wonderful!"

"Where do you want it?" he replied.

I showed him a spot that would be out of the way, but he just laughed.

"That's not nearly big enough."

"How much gravel do you have?"

"Several trucks full."

I'm not sure why it amazes me when God does the magnificent, but with each truck that pulled in and dumped its load near our parking lot, I felt humbled. The Lord showed this company the path to our door, and God supplied what we needed for the base for the barn's ground floor and our parking lot.

On top of that, our original contractor had recommended we put in a heated concrete floor. We had put in the pipes for the heat and poured the cement; however, we really wanted to polish it so the children would have a smooth surface. But by the time we reached this part of finishing the barn, we had nothing left in the budget. That's when God sent a new friend to our rescue.

The quote we received to epoxy and polish the floor was $5,000, but Joe offered to complete the project as a tithe to the Lord. And when he brought his assistant to help with the job, we saw God begin to use the barn to connect people even before we could complete it. Joe's helper just happened to be a friend of Rigo's son. We were blessed to have a beautiful floor and experience the heartwarming reunion.

Another blessing came in the form of our heating and air conditioning units. The HVAC company gave us an estimate of nearly $100,000, but with $10,000 left in the budget, I knew I needed a second opinion. So, I called a friend who has worked in the business for about thirty years. John confirmed the price and asked if I thought we could come up with another $10,000.

"Lamarr, if you can find another $10,000 to pay my crew, I'll purchase all the units you need, and my crew will install them."

"John, that's a huge gift."

"I think the company's tithe for this past year should just about cover it."

Two weeks later, $200,000 worth of HVAC equipment had been installed.

When we LISTEN, God navigates for us. He shows us the path we should take and brings others into our journey to bring His vision to fruition.

Let God Help You as You Navigate

Navigation means continually making progress. Martin Luther King, Jr. said, "If you can't fly, then run. If you can't run, then walk. If you can't walk, then crawl, but whatever you do, you have to keep moving forward." God wants to help you navigate to your higher calling. You were created for something bigger than you can do on your own. The Bible is full of truths that remind us that God wants to lead us and navigate for us.

Following your Godly Positioning System begins with trusting that God always knows the correct path. "Trust in the Lord with all your heart and lean not on your own understanding; in all your ways submit to him, and he will make your paths straight" (Proverbs 3:5-6). We will forever be tempted to lean on our own understanding. Some things in life just make sense. Why wouldn't we simply take that avenue? The problem lies in the fact that when we do what is reasonable, we only see today. God takes us down the path that will be for our best in the future.

Each time we hesitate doing something God invites us to do, we need to ask, "Am I leaning on my own understanding?" Trusting God isn't always easy, but as Henry Blackaby says, "God's commands are designed to guide you to life's very best." God's Positioning System leads us to amazing blessings.

Jeremiah 6:16 tells us how to find that road. This is what the Lord says: "Stand at the crossroads and look; ask for the ancient paths, ask where the good way is, and walk in it, and you will find rest for your souls." We come to crossroads almost daily—points along our path that require us to choose the route we will take. God says to look for the ancient path, the path laid out for all humanity at creation.

God intended us to be in a full, intimate relationship with Him. He wants to be the Light to our path, so we always choose the best way. The key to choosing the right route lies in LISTENing rather than leaning on our own understanding. We have to listen to God when we pray and listen to everything we've learned, especially the things we discovered as we served. Finally, listening to those who inspire and encourage us will help us find the good way. God calls it ancient because He set out the good way before time began. Henry Blackaby recommends we look for the route where we see God at work and follow that path.

LISTEN also means reading scripture and focusing on Christ as we seek the correct route. Psalm 119:105 tells us, "Your word is a light unto my path and a lamp unto my feet." Reading the Bible illuminates the good way. When we walk in the dark, we're more likely to trip and fall. God gave us His word to light our way. On top of that, the Bible tells us that Jesus is the Word (John 1:1) and the Light (John 8:12). Keeping our focus on Christ and His light allows us to see the road more clearly.

It's time to follow God's Positioning System so you can Navigate life and live the abundant life Jesus promises in

Navigate

John 10:10. Scripture, prayer, and finding a mentor or spiritual coach will help you navigate your journey with the fewest bumps and detours. Developing the skills to LISTEN gives us the courage and power to naturally navigate life with the fewest number of obstacles possible. When we walk in the light of Christ, we begin to navigate with the freedom to be everything we were created to be.

8

LISTEN to Unlock Your Higher Calling

Live in the Freedom of Who You Were Created to Be

We live in a world where settling has become the norm. People make excuses for why they've abandoned their dreams. They quit just short of the win. And unfortunately, a bunch of parents have taught their kids that's life. These young people have learned they can quit the baseball team mid-season if it gets too tough, and teachers get blamed for bad grades. Our culture has moved to a place where blame and giving up are touted as the answer to a bad day, but success lies in the opposite direction. It's time to navigate toward ownership and push ahead by learning to LISTEN to unlock your higher calling.

Perhaps we need more mothers like mine. She would not settle for "I lost the check, Mom." No way. Her response was, "Don't come home until you find it." Giving up was not an option. Blaming the other kids for harassing me because I couldn't play basketball was unacceptable. I'm not sure she knew it back then, but her philosophy set me up for success. Before I hit my teen years, I had already developed fortitude. I knew better than to show up at home without whatever it was I was sent after.

LISTEN to Your Vision

Proverbs 2 (RSV) tells us, "My son, if you receive my words and treasure up my commandments with you, making your ear attentive to wisdom and inclining your heart to understanding; then you will understand the fear of the Lord and find the knowledge of God." Solomon understood that in order to really understand God, we needed to LISTEN. And most specifically, LISTEN to wisdom.

Every person has a higher calling—a specific purpose to further the Kingdom of God and something that allows them to walk in the freedom of all they were created to be. In Verse six, Proverbs 2 tells us that the Lord gives wisdom, knowledge, and understanding, but the key to hearing those gems is listening.

Deep down, I always knew the corporate world was not my highest calling, though it was an important part of my journey. I appreciate all I learned and the good living I made that allowed me to make the initial investment in the barn. One of the things we discover as we learn to LISTEN is the difference between the journey and the destination. Sometimes, we allow ourselves to get stuck in our employment or hobbies because we believe we've landed. We don't realize those things are just the legs of the journey. Yes, sometimes they're unnecessary detours—paths we drove down on our own without consulting our GPS. But God will even use those for good. Romans 8:28 promises it.

You might remember I shared that Trevor challenged me to ask, "Who Am I?" During that same weekend, he and I went to breakfast before I headed home. My friend had a few more questions. "Lamarr, I want to know where you see yourself in five years. I'm going to ask you a list of questions and take notes. I'm not going to comment; I'm just going to write." Inquiry after Inquiry—"Describe the farm for me." "What will it look like in five years?" "What will your role be there?"

By the time we were done, he had eight or nine pages of notes. "I'm just going to tuck these away, Lamarr, and we're not going to talk about them for five years."

Sure enough, just before we finished the barn, Trevor came to see me. I showed him around the farm, and he pulled out an envelope.

He said, "Do you remember this, Lamarr."

"Remember what?"

"The notes I took at breakfast five years ago." Page by page, Trevor went through my vision, and as he read, he looked around and started checking things off. We spent about two hours that day going through my answers to his questions. Ninety-eight percent of what he had written, we could now see.

Trevor said, "Lamarr, do you see what has happened over these last five years and what God did with that vision that you just thought you were talking to me about?"

I stood there speechless with tears in my eyes as Trevor continued. "Man, we are standing on your vision right now. All that stuff we talked about—we're here."

God gave me the vision for the barn long before it came to fruition. Fortunately, he also blessed me with a good friend and encourager to help me LISTEN better.

The Lord has a similar vision for you. It probably won't have anything to do with a barn, but if you continue to learn, surround yourself with people who inspire you, serve with all your heart, think about the possibilities, encourage others to find their higher calling, and navigate with God's GPS, He will show it to you.

You Are What You Listen To

Our future is formed by the choices we make on a daily basis. This means that each choice needs to connect to our desires and vision. What we choose to listen to and think about ends up playing a big role in our future. Many times, who or what I choose to listen to prevents me from being the best version of myself.

Sam Dalton mentored me until the day he died. When I was in my late teens or early twenties, he taught me that acronym for fear: False Evidence Appearing Real. He helped me see that many well-meaning people say things in an attempt to protect us. And while their advice sounds prudent, sometimes their ideas are false; however, if it's someone we respect, we're liable to heed their cautionary care. Then, the worst possible outcome becomes real. Oh, it's not that something horrible takes place. The worst possible consequence is that nothing happens.

Fear stops too many people. Sam didn't want fear to ever paralyze me. That's why he gave fear a name. His acronym reminds me that if I experience fear, I know I'm believing some False Evidence. That allows me to step back and ask, "How committed am I to my vision and desires?" I have to choose between the convincing voices that make the False

Evidence Appear Real and the higher calling that sets me free. I decided fear would not paralyze me.

Leaders Listen

Your higher calling will propel you to leadership. You may lead a country like King David, a team as a manager, or a classroom of children as a servant. Regardless of your leadership status, listening may be the most important skill you acquire. Let me say that a bit more simply. Listening is the best form of leadership as you walk toward your higher calling.

When you consider the people who have had the greatest impact on the world, you'll create a list of individuals who knew how to listen. Refusing input from those around us is arrogant and dangerous. Leaders listen to the people closest to them to give them a view of every potential angle of the situation. This puts the leader in a much better position to make the right decision because they have a collaboration of information.

Listening also makes it easier to recruit and retain people to lead. And long story short, if no one is following, you aren't really a leader. You may never know what you do for people when you listen. It shows respect and invites it as well. Listening inspires and instills confidence.

When people feel heard, they want to follow, plus listening gives us an opportunity to engage at a completely different level. As we begin to understand how people feel and think about different subjects, our conversations can go deeper and become more meaningful. Leaders who can communicate on this level make an enormous difference in the lives of those they lead. Additionally, when you're working in your higher calling, this kind of leadership quickly fills your roster so you can navigate to do more and make a greater impact.

Making People Feel Heard

When people feel heard, mountains move, and barns get built. When we listen to someone as they speak, we provide value to that person. That means staying focused. Too often, we listen to respond rather than to hear. When we care enough about others to truly listen, our skills fall into the description of this acronym I designed for the word HEARD.

- H—**Hearing** people has massive implications. Listening means not thinking about what we plan to say next. When we listen so we can speak, we miss the heart of what the other person shares. Listening with the intention to understand and get to know the other person tells them, "I hear you."

- E—**Endless.** The ability to hear others has Endless potential. As people feel heard, they listen more carefully to others. And Endless hearing reminds me I want to enjoy a lifetime of making people feel important and confident by hearing them.

- A—**Appreciate.** The heart of hearing is Appreciating what the other person says as well as the fact that they have a desire to share it with you. When we don't worry about our response, we tell the person, "Let me just Appreciate what you are saying." Much like the message I gave my daughters—even when we don't agree, we can appreciate their ability to share or ask a question.

- R—**Relevance.** When we pause to listen, we send the message that what the other person says has Relevance. It communicates that we value the message as well as the messenger and believe both are important.

- **D—Desire.** Listening says I Desire to listen, and I want to encourage your Desires. When we allow people to feel heard, we tell them we want clarity on their Desires. We want to know the steps they'll be taking to reach their Desires.

Each of us has a higher calling, but in order to unlock it, we must learn to really LISTEN. In the process, we'll also allow others to feel HEARD and make the discovery a double blessing.

Unfortunately, just because you've learned to LISTEN and be present to hear others doesn't mean people will embrace your higher calling. But we can't base our calling on the opinions of the masses. We have to march on following the path God opens for us. While working on the barn, we had several people who couldn't see the vision God showed us.

During that week before our first official worship service in the barn, I contacted that original contractor just like I promised.

"Hey, it's Lamarr from Libertyville. I just wanted to let you know we finished, and we'd love to have you come worship with us this Sunday."

"Wait. You finished that barn project?"

"Yes, sir! And we're having our first service in there this Sunday. Everyone would love for you to come and celebrate with us."

"I'll have to see what I can do. I'm not sure I can make it."

He didn't buy into the vision three years earlier, and I'm not sure he believed we really finished it the way it should have been done. We didn't see him the day of our celebration, but he proved that naysayers can't keep us from carrying out God's vision.

LISTEN to Unlock Your Higher Calling

Celebrate Your Higher Calling

Though we never want to get stuck in a destination, it's important to celebrate the milestones along the way. When we finished our project on the farm, three churches joined us for a huge celebration out on the land. We had a praise band, and hundreds of people came to worship with us.

Before the service, people were milling around, eating, fellowshipping, and having a wonderful time. God gave us a beautiful Saturday afternoon. As I took in the sight, my heart filled with pure joy.

I walked toward Mike and noticed he was crying. "Mike, what's the matter?"

He said, "Pastor, this is everything I dreamed. It's exactly what I wanted when you and I started. I feel like God is so pleased. Look at all these backgrounds and nationalities here today worshiping together."

I gave him a big hug. We were standing on the ramp Mike had designed and poured. The village had come in after all the pavers were laid and told us a ramp would be required to get to the main entrance of the church. Mike had created a beautiful, smooth access next to the stairs Rigo had built. He had grumbled as he built it because he thought it would never get used, and now it was swarming with people. We both felt so blessed by what God had done and the higher calling he had given us.

When the dedication service began, I invited Rigo to lead with me. I spoke in English, and he repeated each sentence in Spanish. I acknowledged Rigo's hard work and gifts to the Lord through Connection Church, and everyone who gathered with us thanked him with rounds of applause. As we unveiled the new street sign, the crowd erupted. The street in front of the church was renamed for Rigo's son. Rosa, Rigo's wife, gasped as I introduced Rigo Jr. Drive. Rigo himself pushed the mic back toward me when I offered it to him to translate those final words. His tears wouldn't let him speak.

Mike, Gabe, Ken, and I watched the remainder of the celebration seated on a stone wall near the barn. We'd started hanging out there after the pounding of hammers and the noise of saws had succumbed to the sounds of birds and nature.

The construction may have been finished, but we knew that just meant the next leg of the journey was about to begin. Some may have called the barn our higher calling. But the barn just gave us a home to carry out our higher calling. Connection Church is on a journey that may outlive me. That may be the best kind of higher calling—something we can continually build and pass along to the next generation. A higher calling continues to grow and help people follow God long after we're gone. We knew the Lord had blessed us, but the completion of the barn was not the end of the story.

PART THREE
Limitless

9

Meet Me at the Barn

Increase Your GPA

Beginning with their freshman year of high school, at least half of the class begins to think differently about their grades. The move from middle school means that class rank and grade point average suddenly become important. Those with a higher GPA have a greater chance of getting into a good college or securing a scholarship.

After much prayer combined with Learning, Inspiration, Serving, Thinking, Encouragement, and Navigation, I have determined that to fulfill my higher calling, I need to help people increase their GPA, but it has nothing to do with grade point average. God has created me to be a Growth Possibilities Accelerator.

The LISTEN model was developed as we completed the work on the barn. It became more than our GPS; it morphed into our GPA. And much like a high grade point average gives some students an advantage when they move on to higher education, those who embrace the Growth Possibilities Accelerator have an increased likelihood of success.

Increasing GPAs has been a major component of Connection Church. We see possibilities everywhere. After watching God open doors and deliver more than we asked for or ever imagined, our congregation understands how to accelerate the possibilities.

Increasing Your GPA through Community

At Connection Church, we want to encourage and help people overcome FEAR so they can take the first step on their journey of walking in the freedom of who God created them to be. We understand that when people begin to see the possibilities as realities and release the chains of limitations, they can increase the speed to reach their goals. The LISTEN model enables people to avoid obstacles and make better decisions because they learn the intricacies of listening to God. The LISTEN model brings Romans 12:2 to the forefront as we learn to discern the good, perfect, and pleasing will of God.

Our congregation especially loves it when folks allow us to walk beside them down their path. A community of like-minded believers is essential to accelerating the possibilities. So, you'll find us in the barn on Sundays and throughout the week, building bonds, mentoring one another, and studying God's Word together.

We understand that distance may keep some from being able to join us on the journey, so we've also created an online community. While we encourage everyone to find face-to-face encounters to push them toward their GPA, we know that some people need more. And with the great gift of connection God has given us through the internet, globally expanding our fellowship is not only possible but also accelerating. We have online communities that focus on marriage, entrepreneurs, those who want to grow in the faith and more. All have one thing in common—they focus on being Growth Possibilities Accelerators for everyone who participates. When you surround yourself with people who Inspire and Encourage and pour yourself into them, you will be amazed at how fast you can Navigate toward making your possibilities realities.

Actions Speak Louder than Words

Workshops, webinars, and courses are just a few ways we encourage people to put the LISTEN model into practice. One of our most popular courses is our Encouraging Marriage Excellence system. Like each of our Higher Calling opportunities, it empowers and inspires participants to live, do, and be the best version of themselves. It doesn't matter how many possibilities we Think; if we neglect Navigating with action, we've already lost.

I love helping people imagine what is possible. Most of us think too small. Humans tend to be protective and act from a "play it safe" mentality. This is the perfect tactic when we're in danger of walking into traffic or jumping from tremendous heights without protective measures. On the other hand, if we're not careful, the same tendencies that keep us from getting hit by a car can limit our potential. Growth Possibilities Accelerator Programs move individuals from limited to limitless and impossibilities to His possibilities.

The world offers boundless opportunities; however, they remain unfulfilled possibilities until someone accelerates them into realities. I want you to believe you can. Philippians 4:13 says, "I can do all things through Christ who gives me strength." And while many people know that verse, their actions demonstrate their interpretation— "I can do some things or most things." It's important to ask yourself, "What do my actions say about what I believe?"

Throughout scripture, we find people who arrived at a crossroads, a place where they had to decide what they believed and what kind of action they would take based on those beliefs. Joshua and Caleb believed that if God was with them, they could conquer all of Canaan. Their belief was so strong they stood up against the other ten spies as well as the entire Israelite community. They didn't back down even when the majority started picking up stones.

David believed God would give him the throne one day, and he believed in God's timing so adamantly that when he had the opportunity to kill Saul and take the throne by force, he refused. Twice, his men wanted to claim what God had promised, but David risked his army deserting when he acted on his belief that the Lord had everything under control.

Jesus' mother believed Gabriel's words. She trusted that God would be with her through the shame and doubt a quick marriage and a short pregnancy would bring. When Gabriel told her nothing was impossible with God, Mary simply said, "May it be done according to Your Word."

These three represent a small sampling of all those in scripture who demonstrated their faith. We know what they believed because of how they lived. Your actions tell the same story, and sometimes, the first person your actions will speak to is yourself. We learn so much about ourselves when we consider the possibilities God puts before us and weigh them against what we see as limits and obstacles. Those potentials for struggle are real; however, by following the LISTEN model, looking to a mentor and a community for support, and diving in deep with an immersive workshop or cohort, we can Navigate over, around, and through those roadblocks into God's limitless power and grace.

Mike's New Journey

Mike was a great example of someone who acted on his beliefs. Though a quiet person of little controversy, when he needed to, Mike stood up against even a good friend to do what he knew God wanted him to do. He followed God to the barn and demonstrated the LISTEN model as he worked. He was constantly learning and was an inspiration and encouragement to everyone he met. Mike thought of possibilities many missed, and as you've seen, he was a true servant.

After our dedication celebration, people stayed and fellowshipped until late in the evening. By the time we cleaned up, everyone was exhausted, and we had to get some sleep so we'd be ready for worship the next morning. I'd only been home a short while when my phone rang. The caller ID said Mike. I thought, *I just talked to him thirty minutes ago.*

"Hey, Mike, what's up?"

"Pastor, I don't think I'm going to get to come to church tomorrow. I think I might have gotten food poisoning today. My stomach hurts really bad. I hate it. It's the first time I've missed it since I started coming. If I'm feeling better, I'll be there, but I just wanted to give you a heads-up in case I don't make it."

"Okay, Mike, just feel better better." I knew he must have been pretty sick to even consider missing worship.

Sure enough, Mike wasn't in church the next day. I planned to check on him on Monday morning, but before I could make the call, a number I didn't recognize showed up on my phone.

"Hello."

"Hello, Pastor?"

"Yes, this is Pastor Lamarr."

"Hi, Pastor, this is Mike's wife. I hope you don't mind. I got your number out of his phone."

"No, no. That's fine. How can I help you?"

"Could you come over here right away? Something happened to Mike."

I left as quickly as I could. By the time I arrived, an ambulance was there. Mike lay on the couch, unconscious. The stomachache had actually been a symptom of a massive heart attack. He had passed away that morning.

Through the tears, Mike's wife asked, "Lamarr, would you do the eulogy? Mike loved you and the church so much." She smiled a bit. "He spent more time with you than he did me."

"I would be honored," I honestly replied.

"And Pastor, would you walk with me through all this? I have to go to the funeral home and take care of everything."

"I'll be there anytime you need me."

As we made the arrangements at the funeral home, the funeral director commented, "I only see one problem with having the service at the barn. I understand your worship center is on the second floor. I'm a little concerned about getting the coffin up there."

I smiled. "You won't believe this, but the last thing Mike did for the barn was design and build a ramp. Getting up there won't be a problem."

All that grumbling Mike did about the ramp, and he was the first one to need it.

The entire time we worked on the barn, Mike talked like it would be his last project. I assumed he thought he might retire, but now I wonder if God had given him a hint of what lay ahead of him.

Mike always hated it when I took his picture or videoed him. But just before the dedication ceremony, I had talked him into letting me video him as he told the story of the barn. For eight minutes, we sat on the stairs, and he shared the story of our relationship and his work at the barn. When I recorded it, I thought it would be great to use for an anniversary someday in the far future. Instead, it made the perfect introduction to Mike's eulogy. Several folks asked me if I knew he was going to pass away. I told them that video was just one more way God took care of every detail.

So many people loved Mike, and Mike loved them right back. But mostly, he loved working for the Lord. Mike found his higher calling by using his master carpentry gifts to bring the barn to life. God gave him the vision of a place where people of all nationalities and cultures would come together to worship and fellowship. Mike followed his higher calling to the end, and now he journeys with Jesus face-to-face.

Now that the barn is complete, I spend my time in the silo. The crew created an office for me in there, and I love it. It's hard not to look around and see Mike in every detail. I think about our late-night coffee sessions. We shared our hopes, dreams, and fears in a way I've never experienced with any other brother-in-Christ.

I feel blessed to have known Mike and called him my friend. God used him to make an imprint on my life as well as the people of Connection Church. The memories he created help fuel our journey.

Mike acted on his higher calling. He poured his belief into creating a place where people can grow in Christ and find their own higher calling. I invite you to LISTEN for God to show you how to accelerate your possibilities and take action so they become realities. And I would be honored to have you stop in at the farm and Meet Me at the Barn.

SMALL GROUP DISCUSSION QUESTIONS

SESSION ONE

Introduction and Chapter One
God Prepared Me for This

On Your Own Before You Meet

    a.   Read the Introduction and Chapter One of this book.

    b.   Make a list of your past experiences. Begin with your childhood and work your way through your adult life. Every memory counts.

    c.   If you have time, read Joseph's story from Genesis 37-50.

    d.   Identify the paragraphs from these two chapters that spoke into your life and be prepared to share.

Introduction and Chapter One God Prepared Me for This

With Your Small Group

1. Invite each person to share the paragraph or sentence from the first two chapters that spoke into their life most loudly.

2. Consider Joseph, Moses, Samuel, David, Joshua, Paul, or your favorite Bible hero. Have at least one-half of the members of the group choose one to share how God prepared him or her for their life journey.

3. Share one or two of your past experiences that prepared you or might be preparing you for your Kingdom work. Which of your experiences most surprised you as preparation potential?

4. Did you relate to any of Lamarr's preparation experiences? If so, which one inspired you the most?

5. Esther from the Bible grew up an orphan in her relative's home. She was a Jew in a foreign country. When Mordecai suggested she be in the running for the next queen, she had adequate reasons to decline. What legitimate obstacles stand in your way?

6. What does Queen Esther's story help us see regarding obstacles? (If members of your group aren't familiar with this Old Testament story, go over the highlights so everyone sees how she became queen and how God used her.)

7. When Haman convinced Xerxes to destroy the Jews in Persia, God had already placed her in the palace so she would have the king's ear. Esther 4:14b (HCSB) says that Mordecai told her, "Who knows, perhaps you have come to your royal position for such a time as this."

How does Esther's story help you have confidence God can do the impossible for you to further His Kingdom?

8. Read 2 Samuel 7:18. What is King David's main question? How would you answer that question, "Who am I?" Write your answer in a notebook so you can refer to it in future sessions.

9. Read Isaiah 55:9. What does this verse mean to you when you consider searching for your higher calling?

10. Read Proverbs 2:6-7. Where do you currently look for wisdom? How do these verses begin to help us transform our thinking about where to find wisdom?

11. Luke 1:37 says, "For nothing will be impossible for God." Replace the word nothing with something that you think is impossible to happen. Perhaps you've never thought about it being impossible for God; however, if you think it is impossible, what does this say about how you view this verse? Memorize this verse this week.

SESSION TWO

Lifelong Learners

On Your Own Before You Meet

    a.   Read Chapter Two: Learn.

    b.   List people God has used to teach you from your childhood until today. What is the most important life lesson you learned from each one? Identify one person who has journeyed further than you who you might invite to mentor you.

    c.   Search for learning opportunities online or in your area. Choose one or two self-study-type learning activities you could add to your schedule. Consider reading or listening to scripture or books, subscribing to a podcast or blog, or enrolling in a self-study course online.

d. Identify the paragraph or sentence from this chapter that spoke into your life.

With Your Small Group

1. Invite each person to share one sentence or paragraph from Chapter Two that spoke into their life.//
2. Read Proverbs 2:1-5. Compare how these verses look at God's commands and words to the way the world views them.
3. What does Proverbs 2:3 tell us is one key to finding wisdom and understanding?
4. In your list of priorities, where do learning and seeking silver fall? (Seeking silver might be the way you earn money.) If you don't consider learning as high a priority as earning money or finding treasure, how can you change that?
5. Read Matthew 11:29-30. A yoke was usually placed on two animals of similar size and pull strength; however, when a young animal needed training, the farmer would have an experienced ox share the yoke with the youngster. It put a strain on the older animal, but the younger learned quickly. How does this imagery help us see the importance of being yoked with Jesus?
6. Read Matthew 28:19-20. How do these verses demonstrate our need for learning? What does Jesus expect us to do with what we've learned?
7. Read Philippians 4:9. What extra benefit of learning does Paul promise?

8. Invite each member to share at least one learning experience they listed on their own. How might that learning experience help someone in the group find peace?

9. How does learning raise the bar on our understanding of Luke 1:37 (For nothing will be impossible for God.)?

10. How could keeping your ears and mind open to learning help you answer the question, "Who am I?"

SESSION THREE

Find Inspiration

On Your Own Before You Meet

    a.   Read Chapter Three: Inspire.

    b.   Make a list of those who "have your ear." Circle those who bring inspiration to your life. Pray about the ones you didn't circle. Are there members of your church or small group who you should add to this list so they can inspire you more often?

    c.   Which sentence or paragraph from Chapter Three inspired you most?

Find Inspiration

With Your Small Group

1. Invite each person to share the most inspirational quote from Chapter Three.
2. Proverbs 2:2 tells us to turn our ears toward wisdom. How can you do that more effectively?
3. What do you look for in a person you allow to influence your life?
4. Read Jeremiah 29:11. How does Jeremiah's message inspire you?
5. How does the acronym for FEAR (False Evidence Appearing Real) put fear in the proper perspective?
6. Read Romans 8:28. How can Paul's words help you combat the fear that blocks inspiration?
7. Read 1 Peter 5:7. How do you cast your anxieties on Jesus? How far can you cast them?
8. Read Exodus 18:13-26. How did Jethro inspire Moses? How did this help him as he traveled through the desert for forty years? How might it have inspired the entire community of Israel?
9. Moses needed a team, but he was also an inspiration to his countrymen. Who do you inspire?
10. How can an inspiring team help you discover who you are?

SESSION FOUR

Self-Sacrificing Service

On Your Own Before You Meet

a. Read Chapter Four: Serve.

b. Make a list of your passions, talents, and abilities. Ask the leaders of your church for a list of all the ways to serve within the church, even those positions already filled. Which of your passions, talents, or abilities could help with one or more of those areas of ministry?

c. Explore ways to serve outside your local congregation. Create a list of organizations that need servants of Christ to help.

d. What paragraph or sentence spoke to you the most as you read this chapter?

Self-Sacrificing Service

With Your Small Group

1. Invite each member of the group to share the paragraph or sentence that spoke to them most clearly as they read Chapter Four.

2. Ask each member to share one passion, talent, or ability they listed.

3. Read Joshua 24:14 & 15. What "gods" get in our way of serving today?

4. Most people don't think of jobs, children, sports, television, and electronics as gods, but we often allow them to take the time we would otherwise devote to God. What adjustments would you need to make in your life to be able to say, "As for me and my house, we will serve the Lord"?

5. Read Ephesians 6:7-8. What does it mean to act as if you were serving God rather than men?

6. What could you change as you work in your current occupation so you are serving God rather than men? What about other areas of your life?

7. Read Galatians 5:13. What's the difference between using your freedom to indulge your sinful desires (flesh) and serving others? What does it mean to serve them with humility? How is this different than serving for recognition?

8. How does getting dirty in service tie in with humility? What limit do you put on how dirty you'll get to serve?

9. What excuses have you used to avoid service? Which of these excuses are born of fear?

10. How does the acronym False Evidence Appearing Real help you put fear in the proper perspective?
11. What do Proverbs 2:7 and Luke 1:37 do to fear?
12. How do getting dirty, giving up excuses, and not succumbing to fear add to the sacrifice involved in service? What other sacrifices does service require?
13. What kind of service do you think you should continue with or try next? How can serving help you answer the question, "Who am I?"

SESSION FIVE

Think About the Possibilities

On Your Own Before You Meet

    a.   Read Chapter Five: Think.

    b.   Make a list of things you've considered doing for Christ that seemed impossible.

    c.   For at least six days, write down at least two positive things you saw or ways God worked during the past twenty-four hours.

    d.   Which paragraph or sentence spoke to you most in Chapter Five?

With Your Small Group

1. Have each person share the paragraph or sentence that spoke to them most and why.

2. How did forcing yourself to write down two positive things each day change the way you looked at things, if at all?

3. Read Luke 1:26-38. How much of what Gabriel told Mary would have seemed possible to the young woman? How would Mary have viewed being highly favored while in poverty, God being with her, having a child, the child being God's Son, or giving birth to a child that would reign over all Israel forever?

4. What was Mary's first and second response? What do they show about her belief in the impossible?

5. Read Colossians 3:2. How did Mary set her thoughts on things above? Look at the list you made on your own this week. How many of those items seem more possible when you set your sights on things above?

6. Read 1 Peter 1:13. How does a fully sober and alert mind help? How does this description fit Mary's mind? When you consider Mary's responses, do you think being sober and alert means we ignore reality? What then?

7. Read Romans 12:2. What kind of thinking conforms to the pattern of this world? What do you do that renews your mind, or what would you like to put into practice to renew your mind?

8. Invite at least two people to bravely share: Which of your impossible tasks requires additional learning?

Think About the Possibilities

How can you acquire this knowledge? Do others in your small group have ideas?

9. Invite at least two people to bravely share: Which of your impossible tasks could use an inspirational team?

10. Invite at least two people to bravely share: Which of your impossible tasks involve service?

11. Which of the impossible tasks on your list would you most like to see happen if nothing is impossible?

12. How can thinking about the possibilities help define who you are?

SESSION SIX

Encouragement Helps Us LISTEN

On Your Own Before You Meet

    a.   Read Chapter Six: Encouragement.

    b.   Make a list of those who have given you encouragement through the years. Consider schoolteachers, counselors, mentors, youth leaders, coaches, and more. Beside each name, write how they encouraged you or what their encouragement prompted you to do.

    c.   Make a second list of those you meet at least monthly who need encouragement. Include the people who seem

Encouragement Helps Us LISTEN

to have it all together as well as those who don't have much courage to share.

d. Select a paragraph or sentence from Chapter Six that gave you the greatest encouragement.

e. OPTIONAL: Read 1 Samuel 17, Daniel 3, and Daniel 6 and prepare answers for questions four through six below.

With Your Small Group

1. Invite each person to share the sentence or paragraph that gave them the most encouragement.

2. Allow each person to tell the group about one person who encouraged them in their youth.

3. Read 1 Samuel 17, Daniel 3, or Daniel 6 (If you have a large group, break into three small groups and let each read one of the passages.)

4. What did David, Daniel, and his friends learn about God during their trial?

5. What did they do about the things that seemed impossible?

6. How do their stories encourage you?

7. How can reading scripture more often be an encouragement to you?

8. Read Joshua 1:9, Isaiah 40:31, and 1 Thessalonians 5:11. How do these three verses provide encouragement?

9. How is encouragement driven by love? How can encouragement fulfill Jesus' command to love others?

10. How can you direct encouragement at fear? How does Paul use encouragement to defeat fear in 2 Timothy 1:7?

11. How has encouragement transferred strength to you in the past? How did God transfer His power in Joshua 10:7-8?

12. How can encouraging others lead you to the truth about who you are?

SESSION SEVEN

Navigate Toward Your Higher Calling

On Your Own Before You Meet

    a.   Read Chapter Seven: Navigate.

    b.   Life is a journey. Record the mile markers you've passed so far, memories, encounters you've had with Christ, and experiences that showed you which way to go next.

    c.   Which sentence or paragraph spoke to you most from this chapter?

With Your Small Group

1. Ask each group member to share the sentence or paragraph that spoke to him or her the most.

2. Read these verses from 1 Samuel: 16:13, 16:21-22, 17:50, 18:2, 18:5, 18:12-13, 19:10, and 23:9, and these from 2 Samuel: 1:1, 5:1-4, 7:8, 11:4-5, 11:27, and 23:1. What obstacles did David navigate? How did they help him reach his higher calling?

3. Read Psalm 119:105. God's Word is a light. What is the value of a light in navigation? What does this tell us about scripture?

4. Read Proverbs 3:5-6. Good navigation means taking the right path. How can we be sure our paths are straight?

5. How is leaning on our own understanding like ignoring our GPS when it tells us which way to turn?

6. How can you acknowledge God in all you do? How does this tie to Ephesians 6:7-8 that we talked about in our Serving session?

7. Read Proverbs 2:2-7. How does turning your ear toward wisdom and the promises of these verses confirm the fact LISTENing does not mean agreeing?

8. Read Proverbs 6:16. When navigating, we often come to a crossroads. The ancient path refers to the road God laid out at creation. How is the ancient path the good one? What does God promise for us when we take the correct path?

9. Who has God navigated your way to help you in your quest to find the freedom to be everything God created you to be?

10. Now that you've made it to the "N" in LISTEN, how would you answer the question, "Who am I?"

SESSION EIGHT

LISTEN to Unlock Your Higher Calling

On Your Own Before You Meet

    a. Read Chapter Eight: LISTEN and Chapter Nine: Meet Me at the Barn.

    b. Make a list of those who speak into your life. Circle the ones who speak positivity into your life.

    c. How would you answer the question, "Who am I?"

    d. Which sentence or paragraph from these chapters spoke to you?

LISTEN to Unlock Your Higher Calling

With Your Small Group

1. Invite each participant to share the sentence or paragraph that spoke to them the most.

2. How can each letter in the LISTEN model help you navigate toward your higher calling?

3. Read Proverbs 15:22. What instruction does God give us in Proverbs about who we listen to?

4. Dissect the letters and the definitions of HEARD. Discuss ways you can put these five practices in place to allow you to listen better.

5. What Godly possibilities have you uncovered as you progressed through these discussions?

6. Read Philippians 4:13. To what degree do you embrace Paul's words?

7. How can the LISTEN model accelerate those possibilities and increase your GPA?

8. What have you discovered about yourself and your higher calling as you've moved through this study?

9. How can you begin to follow your higher calling?

Acknowledgments

As I pen these words of gratitude, I am filled with profound appreciation for the individuals and entities whose support and guidance have played an instrumental role in bringing this book to fruition.

First and foremost, I pay homage to my late mentor, Evangelist Sam Dalton. Your wisdom, encouragement, and unwavering belief in my potential have left an indelible mark on my journey. Your legacy lives on in the pages of this book.

Heartfelt thanks to Igniting Souls publishers for their commitment to fostering transformative ideas and for believing in the power of storytelling. Kary O, your guidance and expertise have been invaluable in navigating the intricate path of publishing, and I am truly grateful for your partnership.

Acknowledgments

To Lynn and Jill, whose editorial insights and dedication have shaped this manuscript into its best form, I extend my deepest appreciation. Your keen eye and thoughtful suggestions have been a guiding light.

Dan Sullivan and the entire team at Strategic Coach, your innovative thinking and strategic frameworks have been a source of inspiration. Thank you for challenging me to stretch beyond my limits and for providing the tools to achieve my full potential. Roderick and Kim Liptrot thanks for not only believing in our vision but supporting it every step of the way. Words cannot express my gratitude.

A special acknowledgment goes to Connection Church, Curtis Evans, Joe Webb, Peter Trevor Wilson, and Gina Johnson for fostering a community of support and encouragement. Your prayers and encouragement have been a source of strength.

Lastly, I acknowledge The One who makes all things possible—my Lord and Savior Jesus Christ. Your grace, guidance, and unending love have been the bedrock of my journey. This book is a testament to the blessings and inspiration that flow from your divine presence.

To each of you, I express my deepest gratitude. This book stands as a collective effort, and your contributions have made it possible for my words to reach the hearts and minds of readers.

About Lamarr K. Lark

Lamarr Lark is a co-founding pastor of Connection Church in Libertyville, IL. As a visionary who loves turning vision into practical leadership strategies, he owns and operates the Gurnee Chick-fil-A in Gurnee, IL. There, he works to help build and strengthen the brand of Chick-fil-A in the Chicagoland market.

As a former Divisional Vice President of Human Resources at Abbott and a seasoned executive with over 25 years of corporate experience, he has been recognized by many local and national organizations for his leadership

About Lamarr K. Lark

contributions to work-life balance, diversity, and strategic human resource planning. In addition to his corporate career, he served his country with distinction and held the rank of Captain in the US Army Reserve.

Lamarr earned his BS from Grace College & Theological Seminary in Winona Lake, IN, where he sits on the Grace Schools Board of Trustees. He also is a former Board member of Converge Mid-America. He is an acknowledged advisor, author, and speaker on human resource strategies, diversity/inclusion, and human equity.

Lamarr and his wife, Brenda, have been married for over 35 years. They are the proud parents of 3 adult children.

Connect with Lamarr at ReachMyHigherCalling.com.

Higher Calling

An exlusive marriage program for high-acheiving couples looking to reach new hights together.

Empowering couples with the vision, tools, and robust support system to transform their marriage from its current state to its intended flourishing destination.

ReachMyHigherCalling.com

THIS BOOK IS PROTECTED INTELLECTUAL PROPERTY

The author of this book values Intellectual Property. The book you just read is protected by Easy IP™, a proprietary process, which integrates blockchain technology giving Intellectual Property "Global Protection." By creating a "Time-Stamped" smart contract that can never be tampered with or changed, we establish "First Use" that tracks back to the author.

Easy IP™ functions much like a Pre-Patent™ since it provides an immutable "First Use" of the Intellectual Property. This is achieved through our proprietary process of leveraging blockchain technology and smart contracts. As a result, proving "First Use" is simple through a global and verifiable smart contract. By protecting intellectual property with blockchain technology and smart contracts, we establish a "First to File" event.

Powered By Easy IP™

LEARN MORE AT EASYIP.TODAY

www.ingramcontent.com/pod-product-compliance
Lightning Source LLC
Chambersburg PA
CBHW052143070526
44585CB00017B/1949